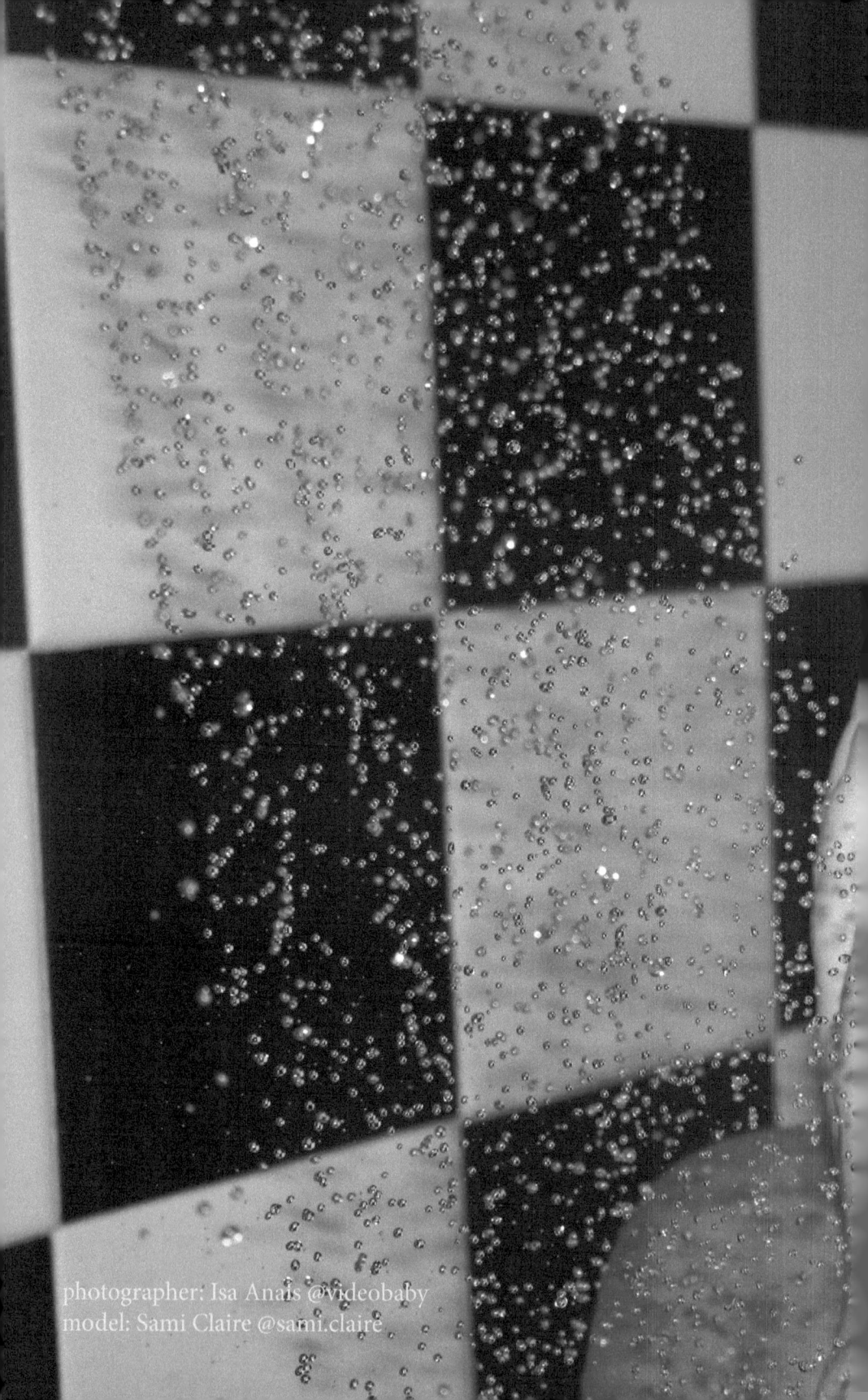

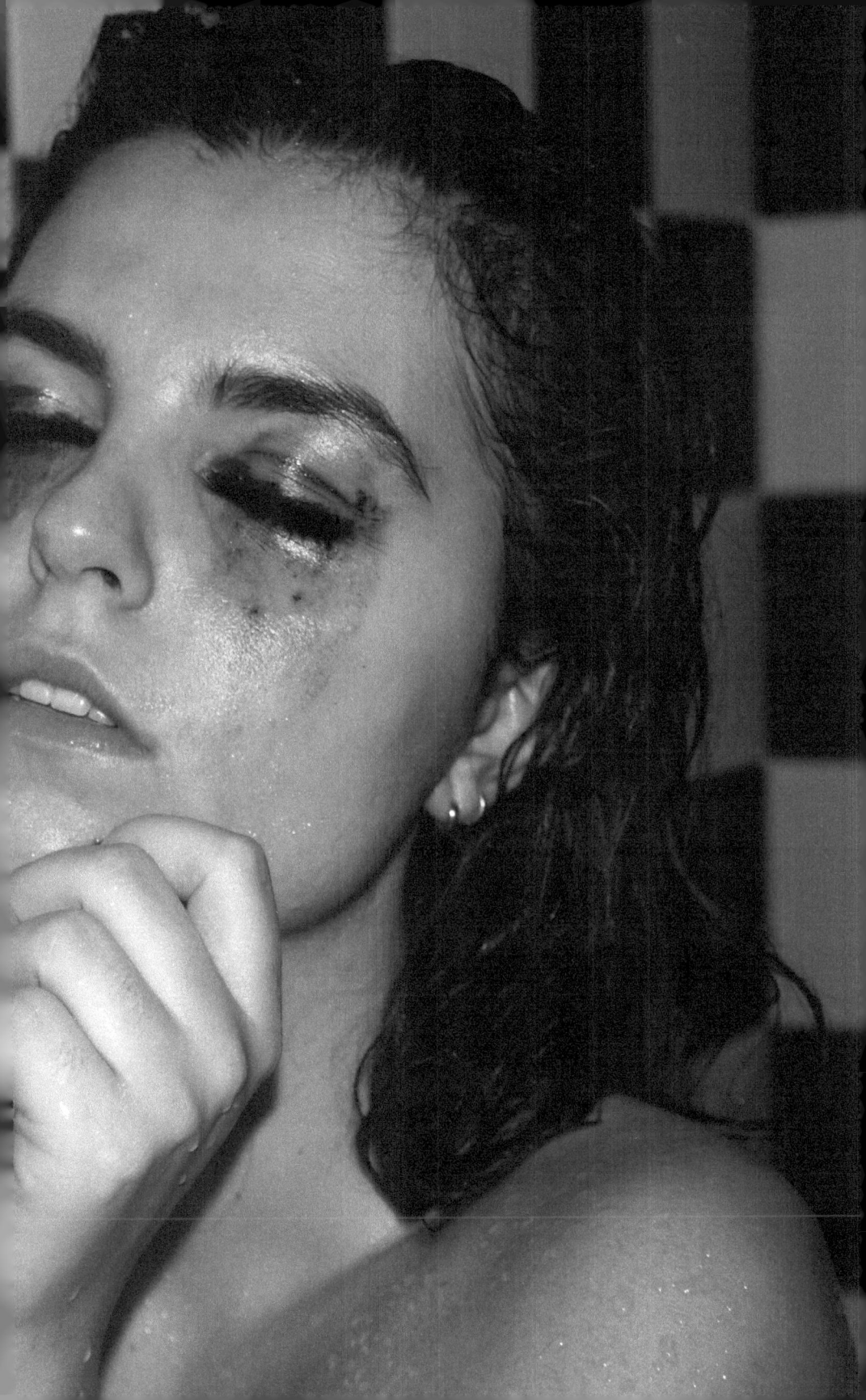

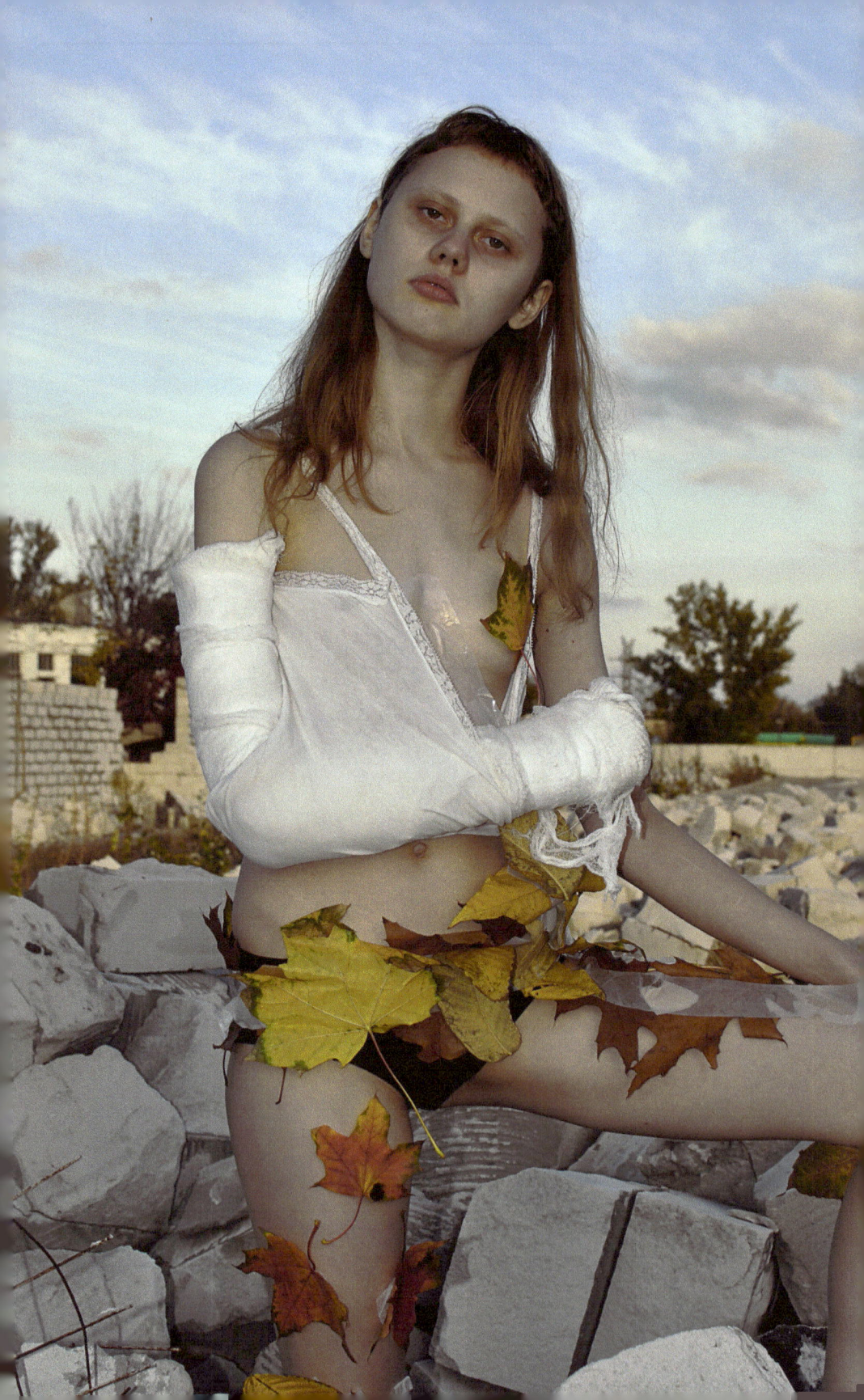

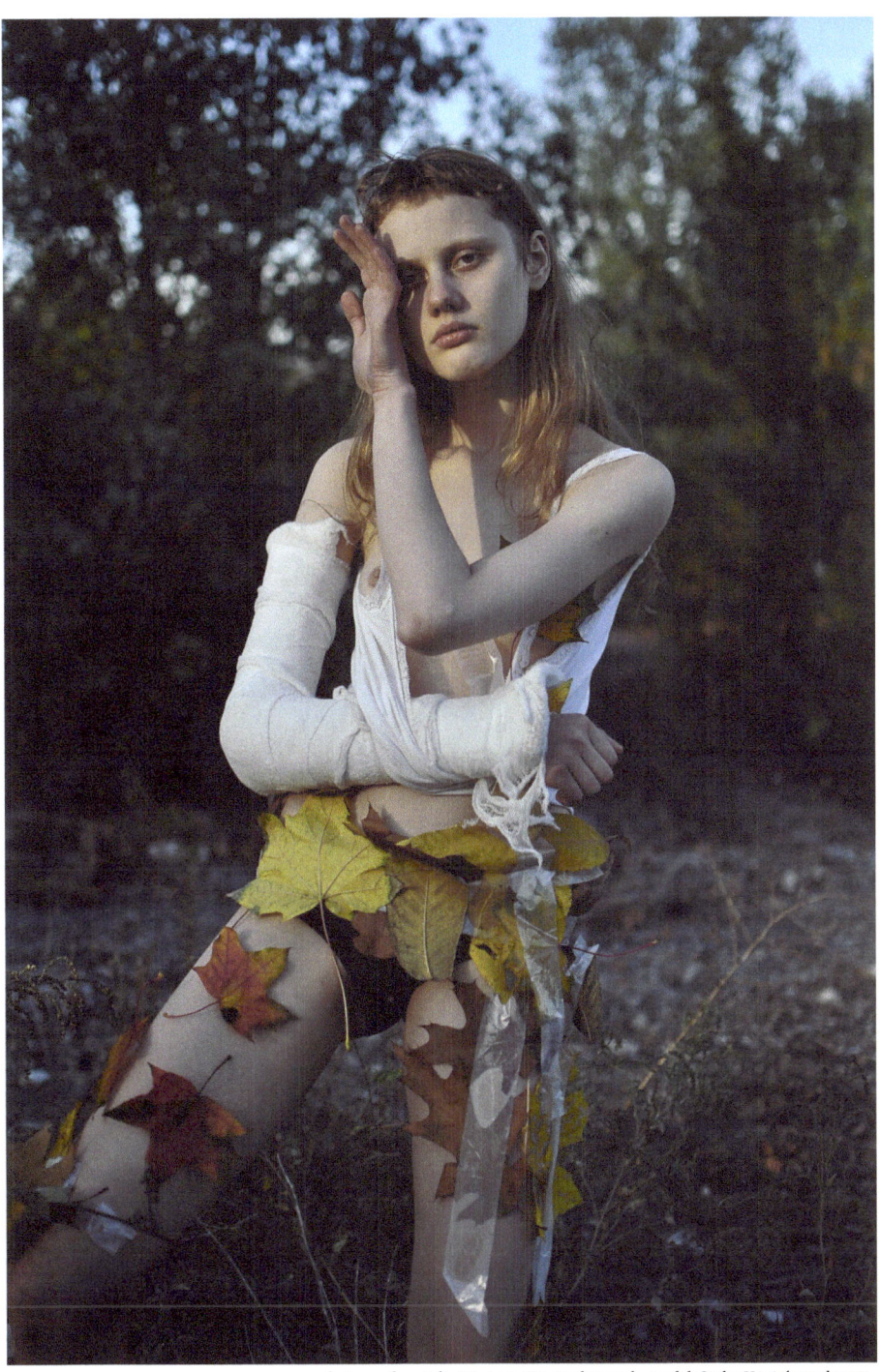

photographer: Julia Martova @yesterdaisygirl   model: Sasha Yatsiuk @zzhvann

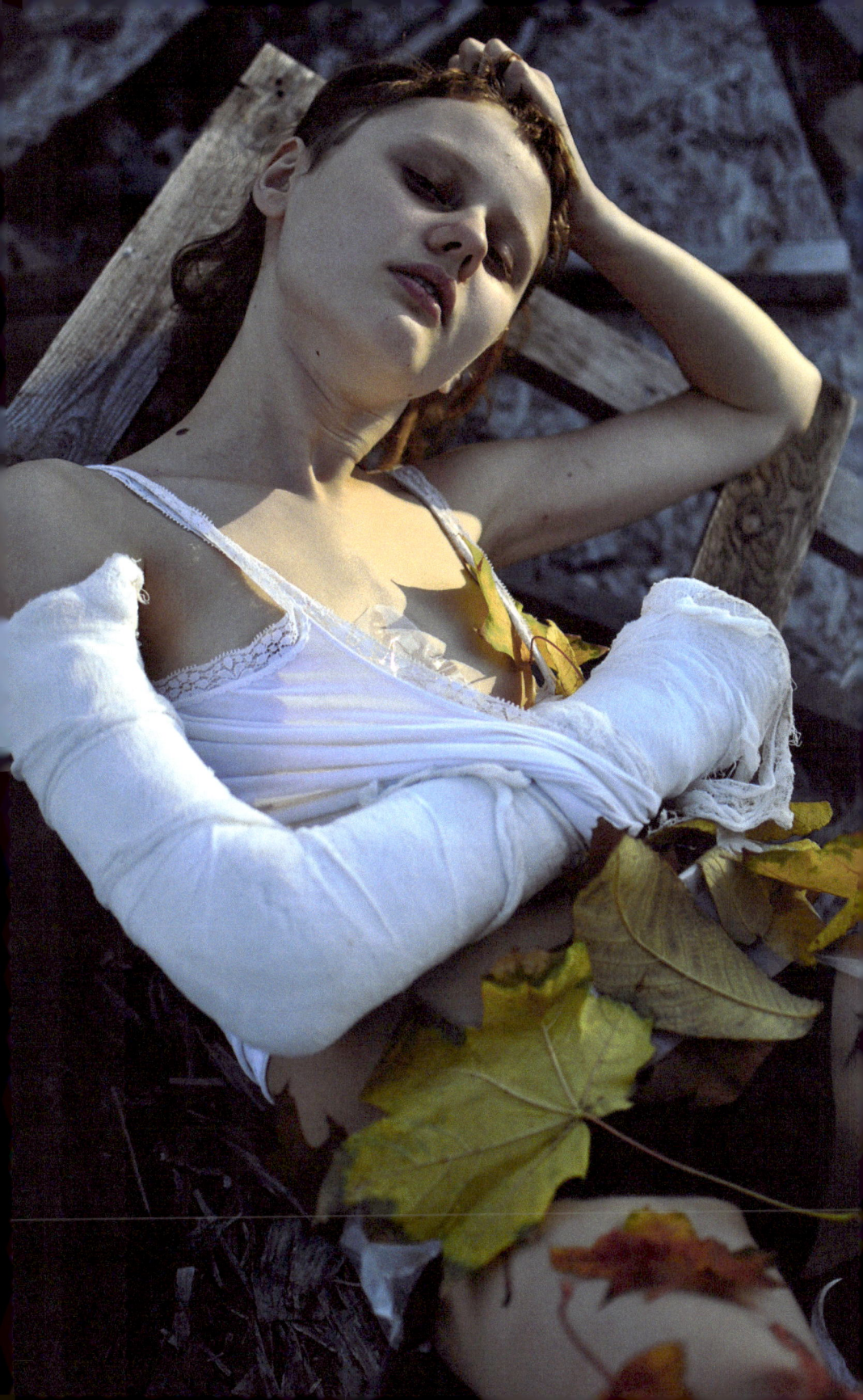

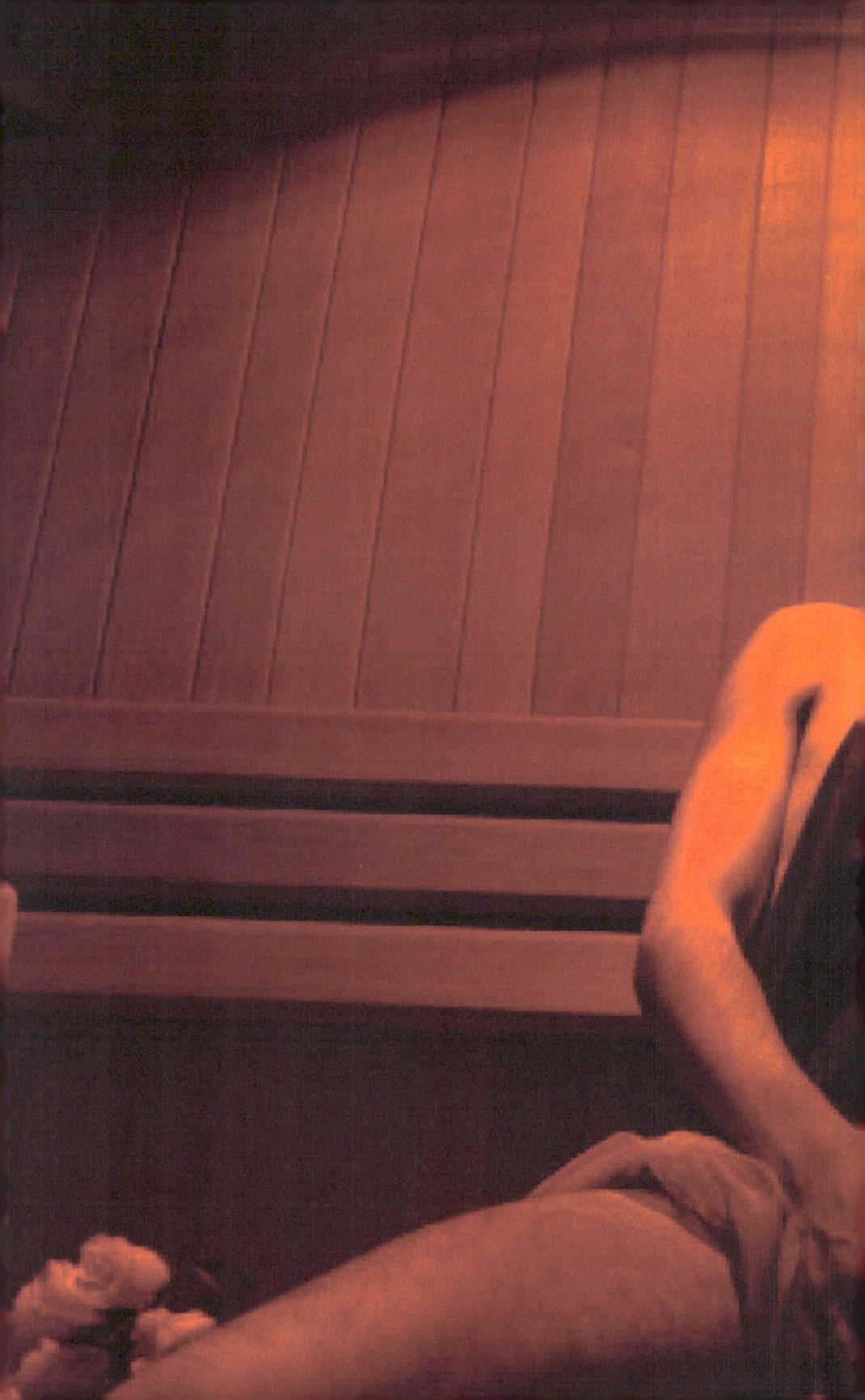

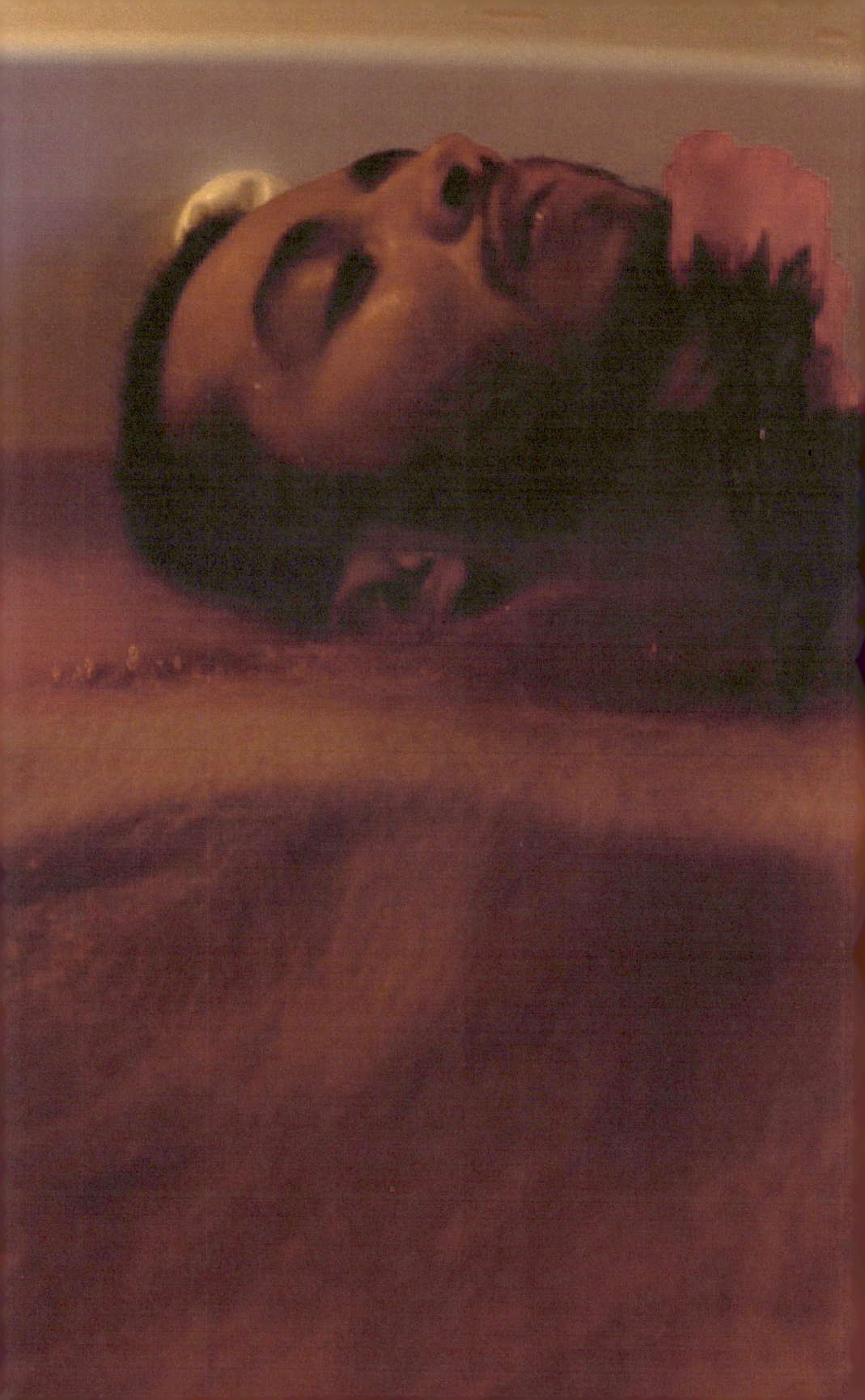

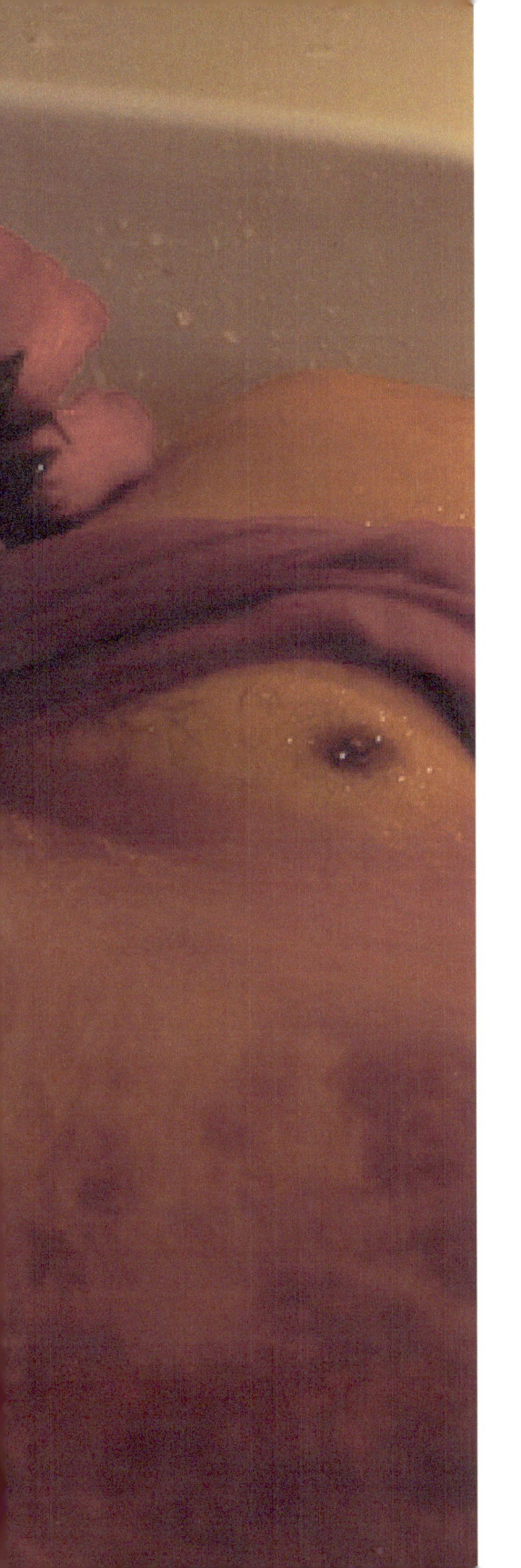

photographer: @berandea_

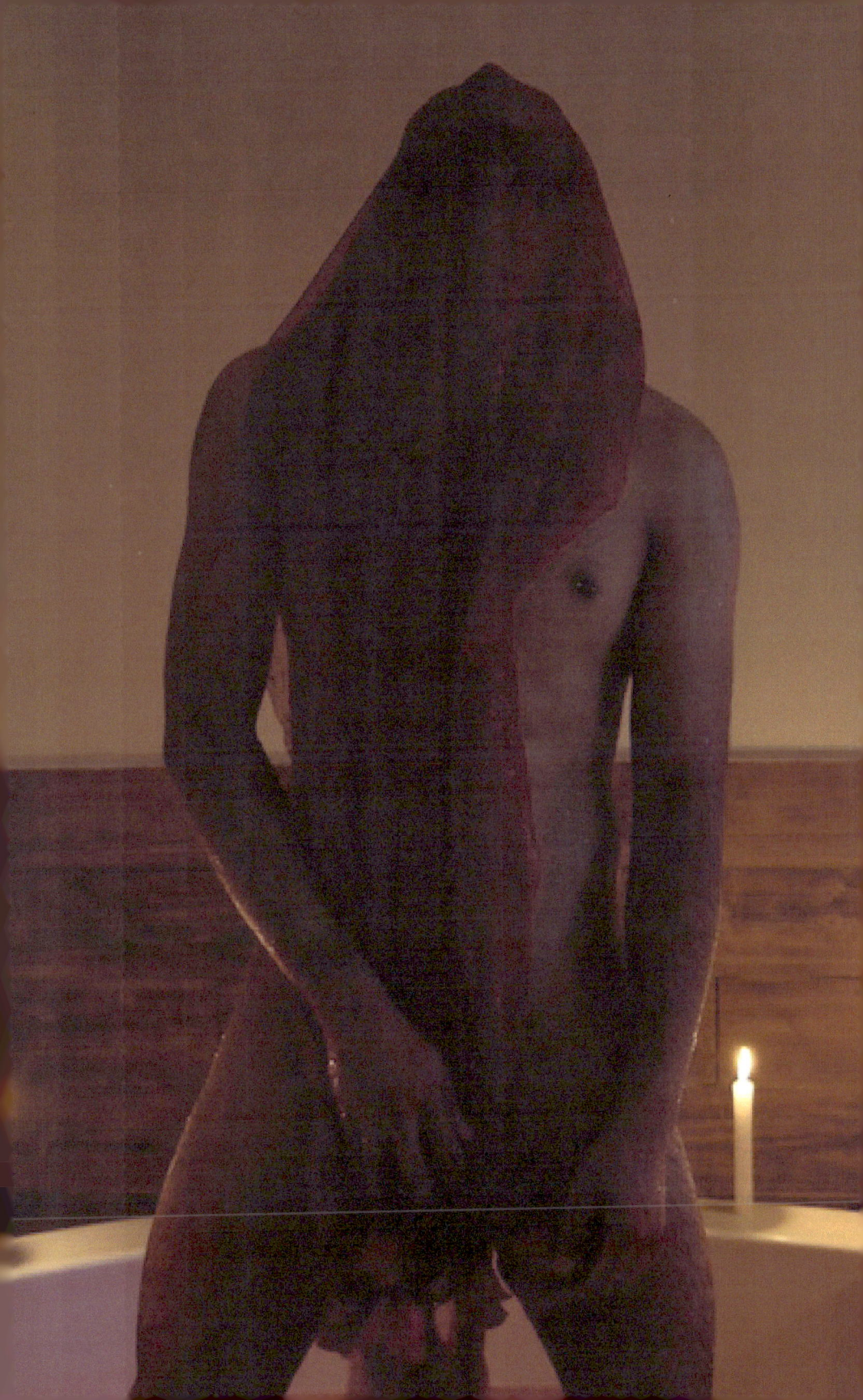

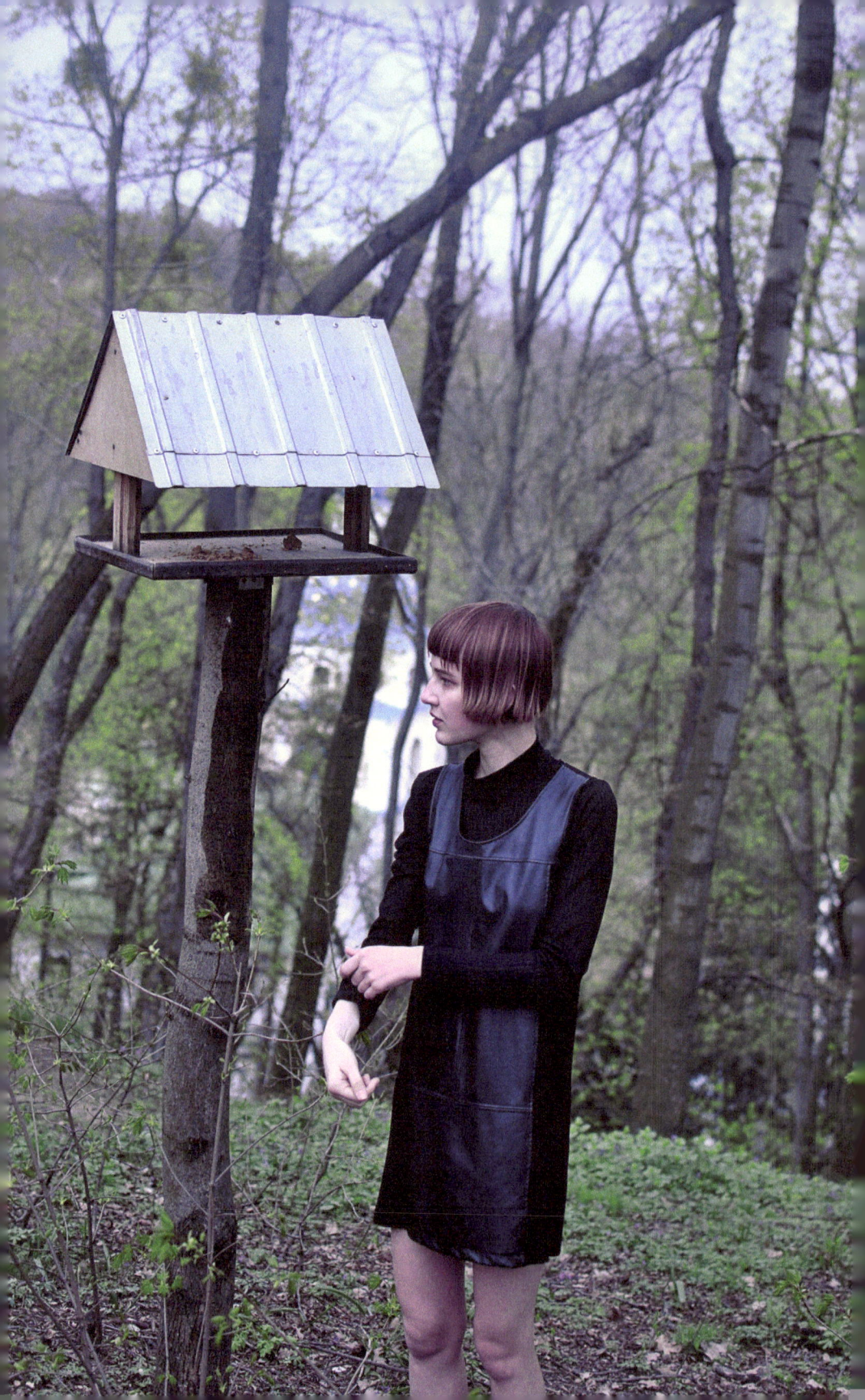

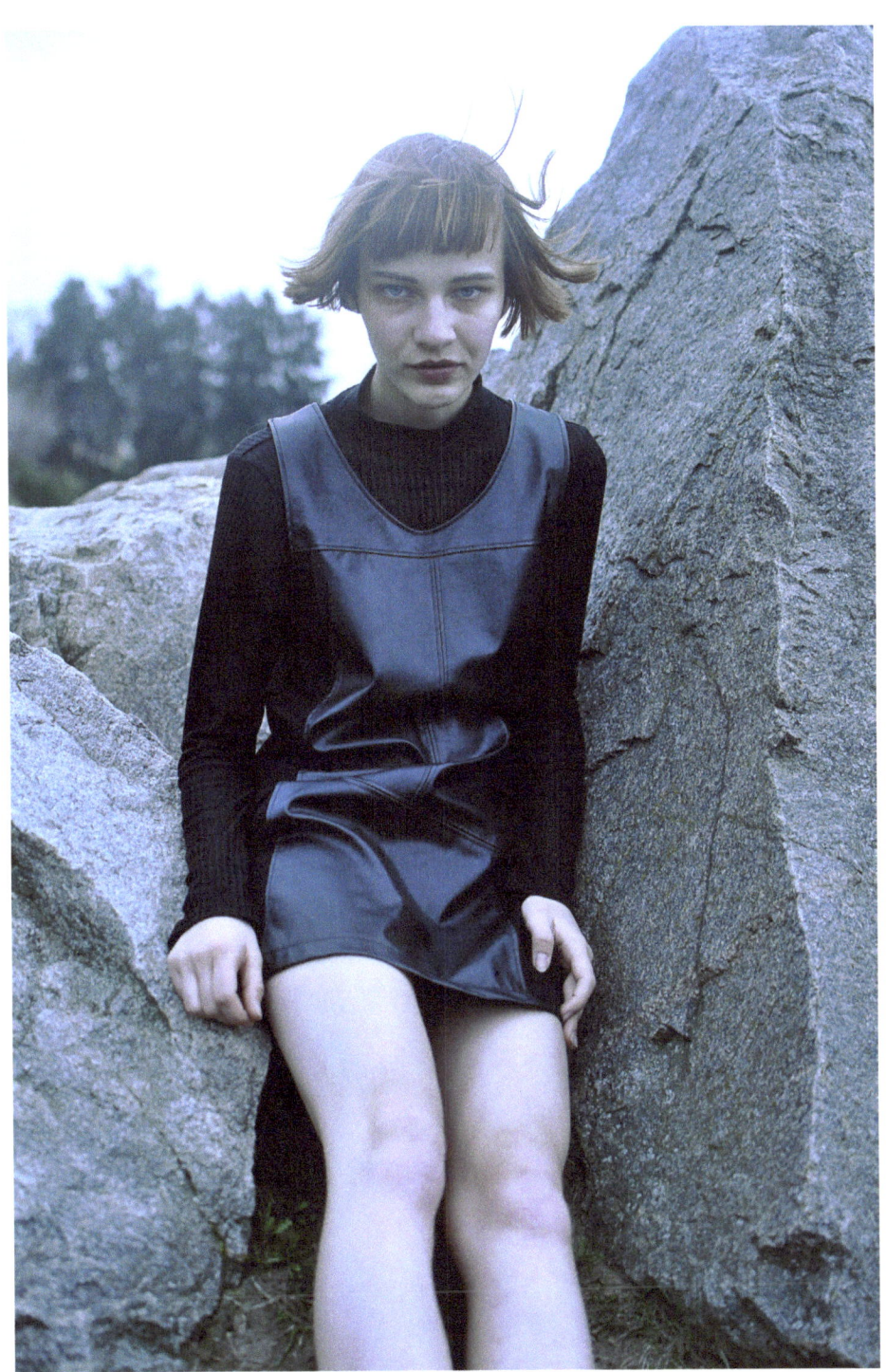

photographer: Julia Martova @yesterdaisygirl   model: Tania Sove @privetik84

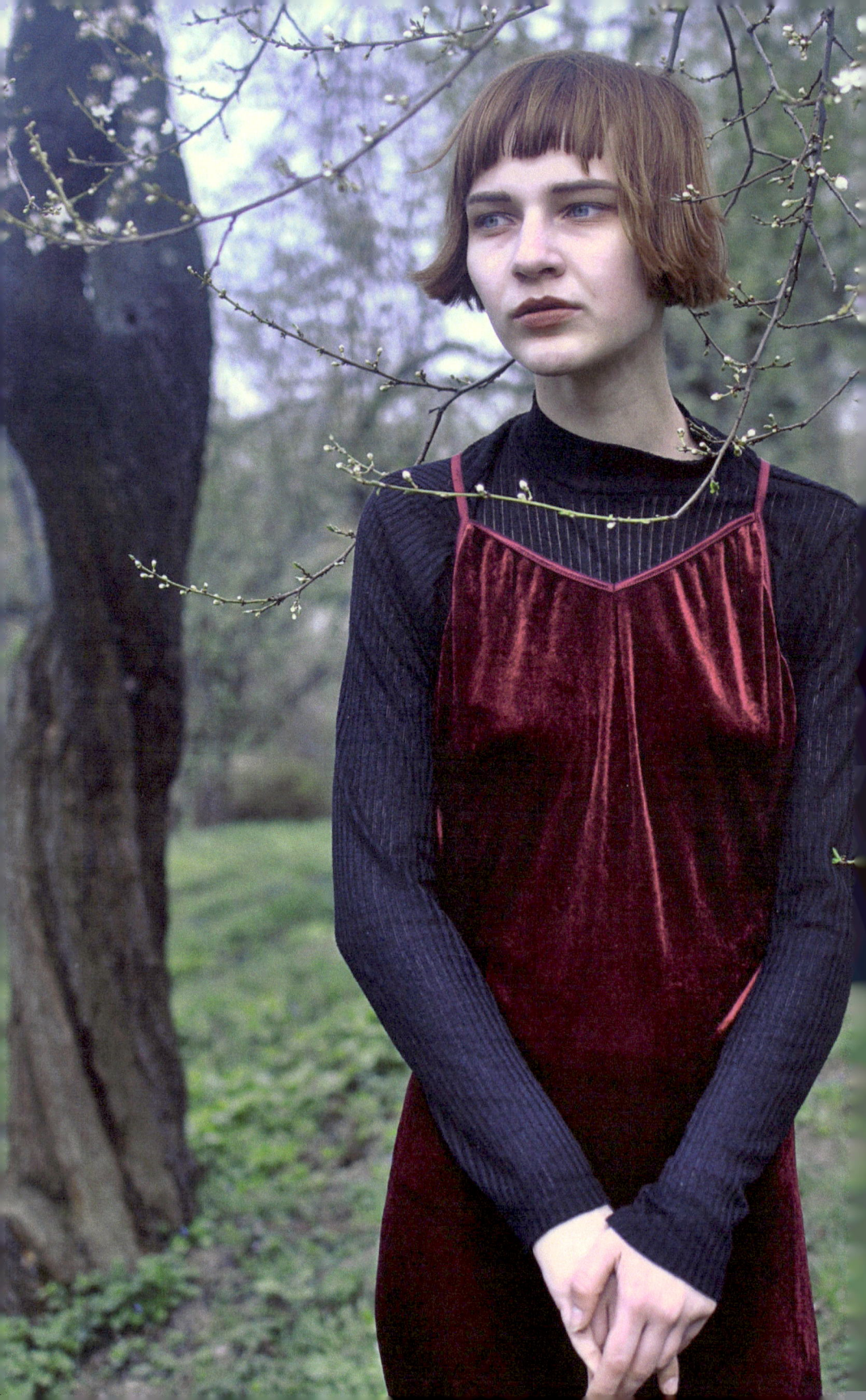

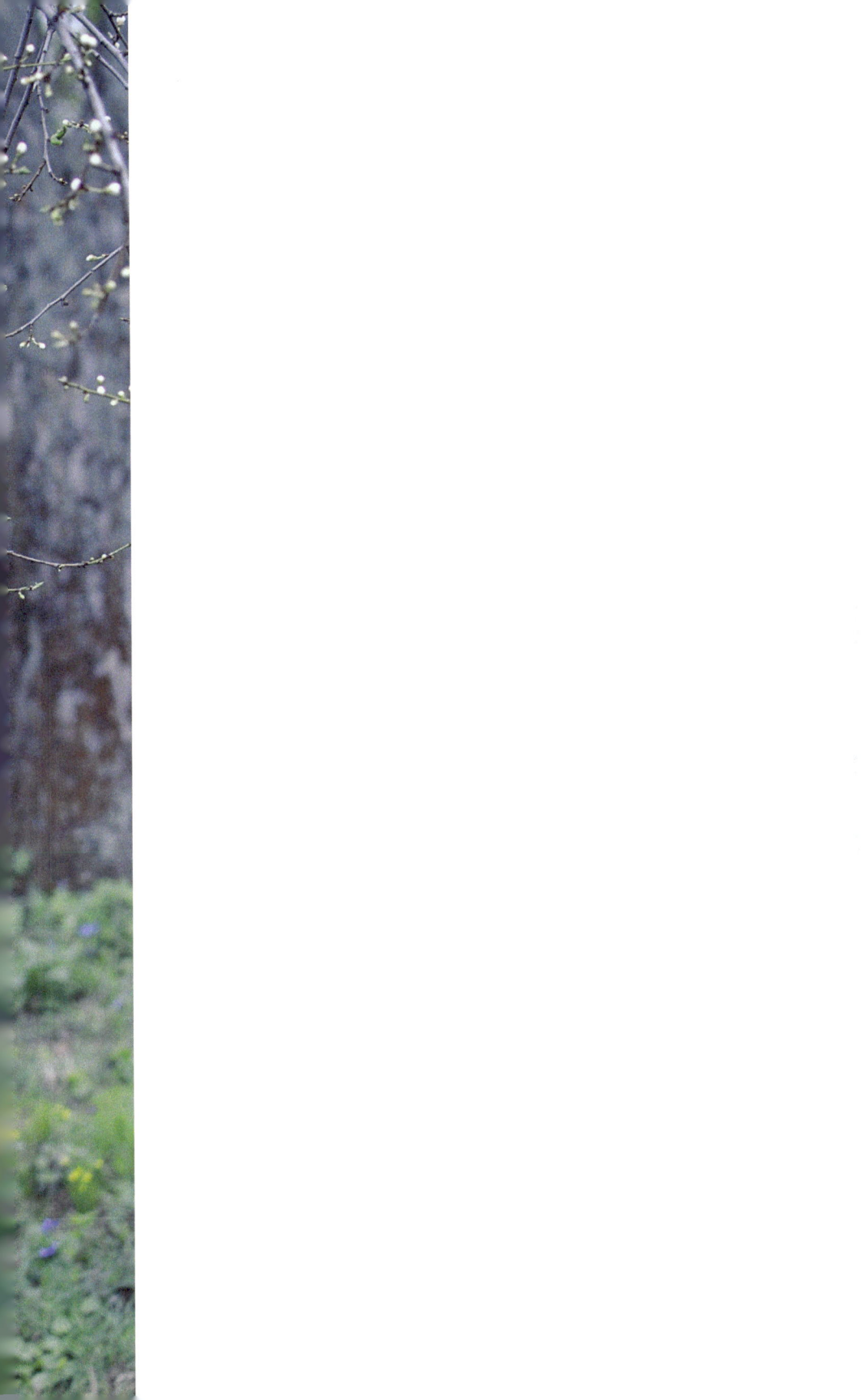

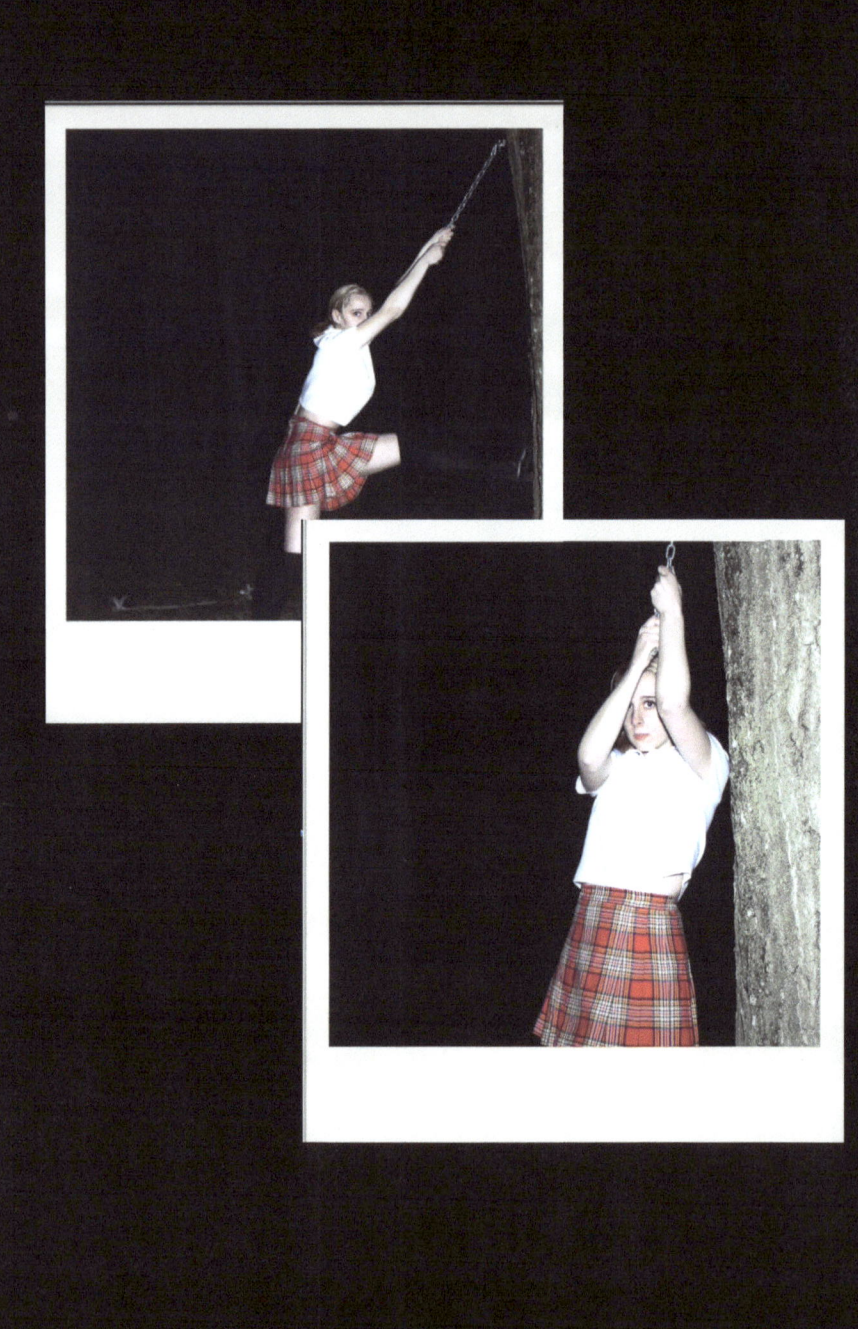

photographer: Isa Anais @videobaby
model: Sarah Isaacs @helado_baby

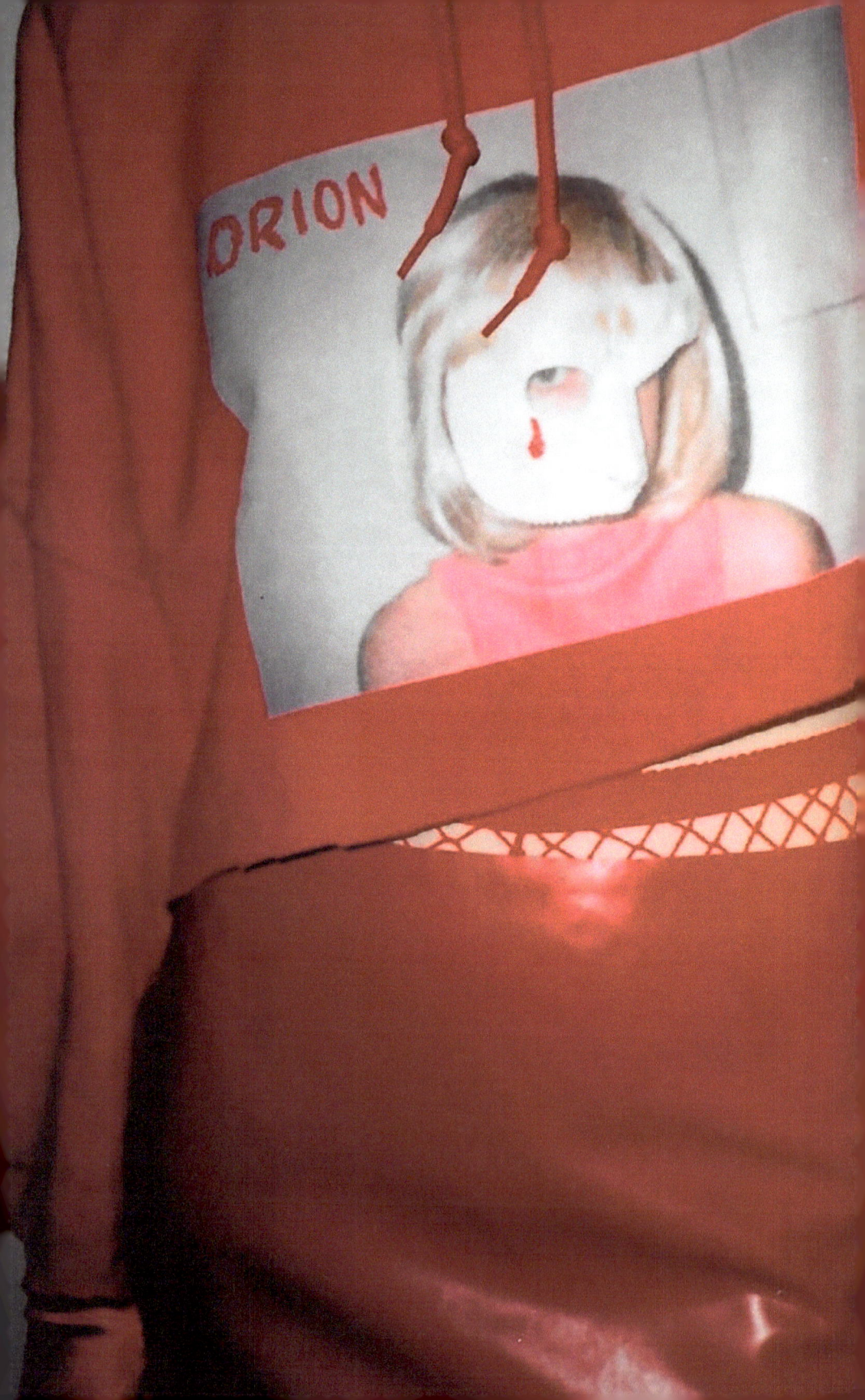

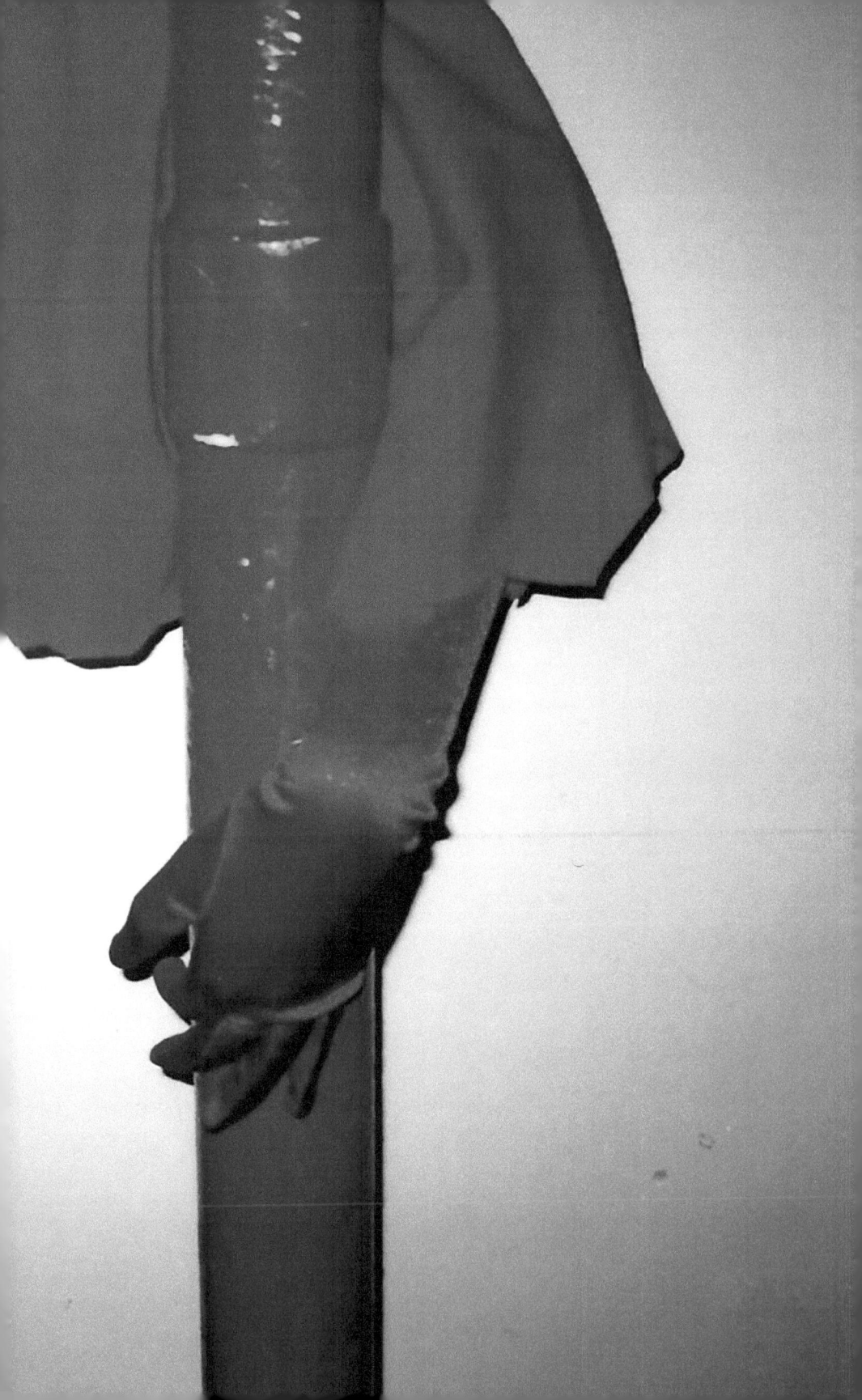

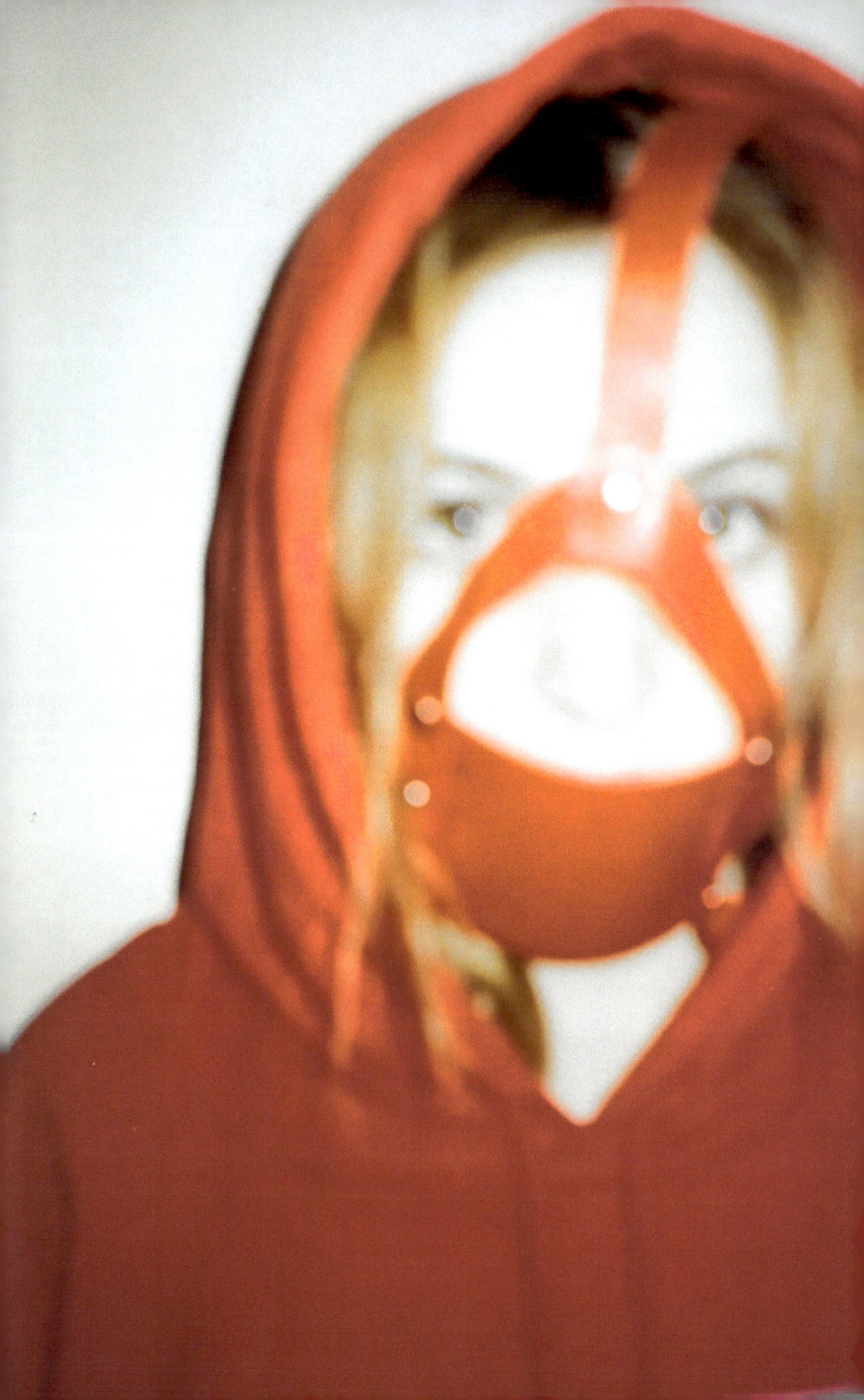

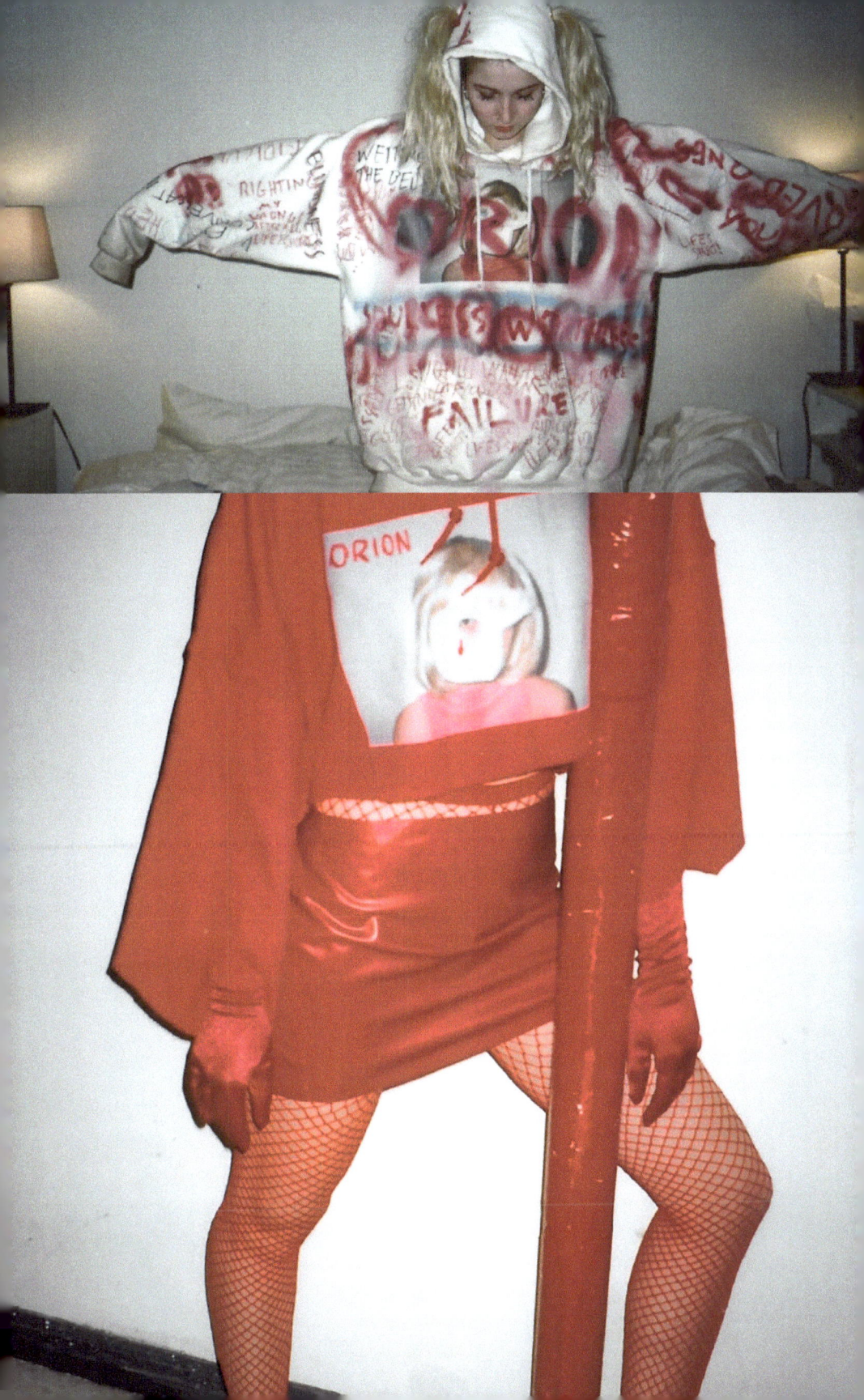

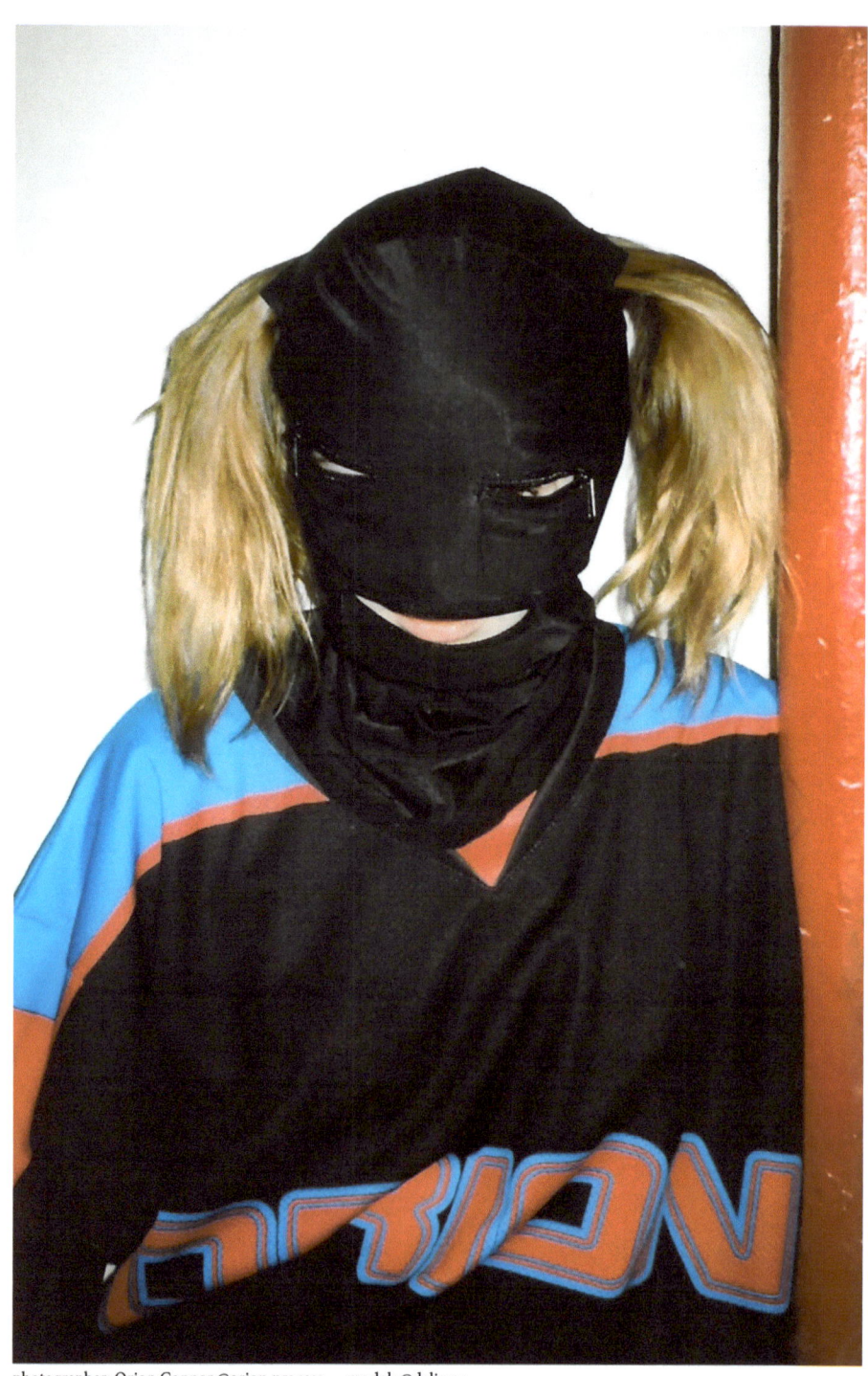

photographer: Orion Connor @orion.process   model: @delia.gc

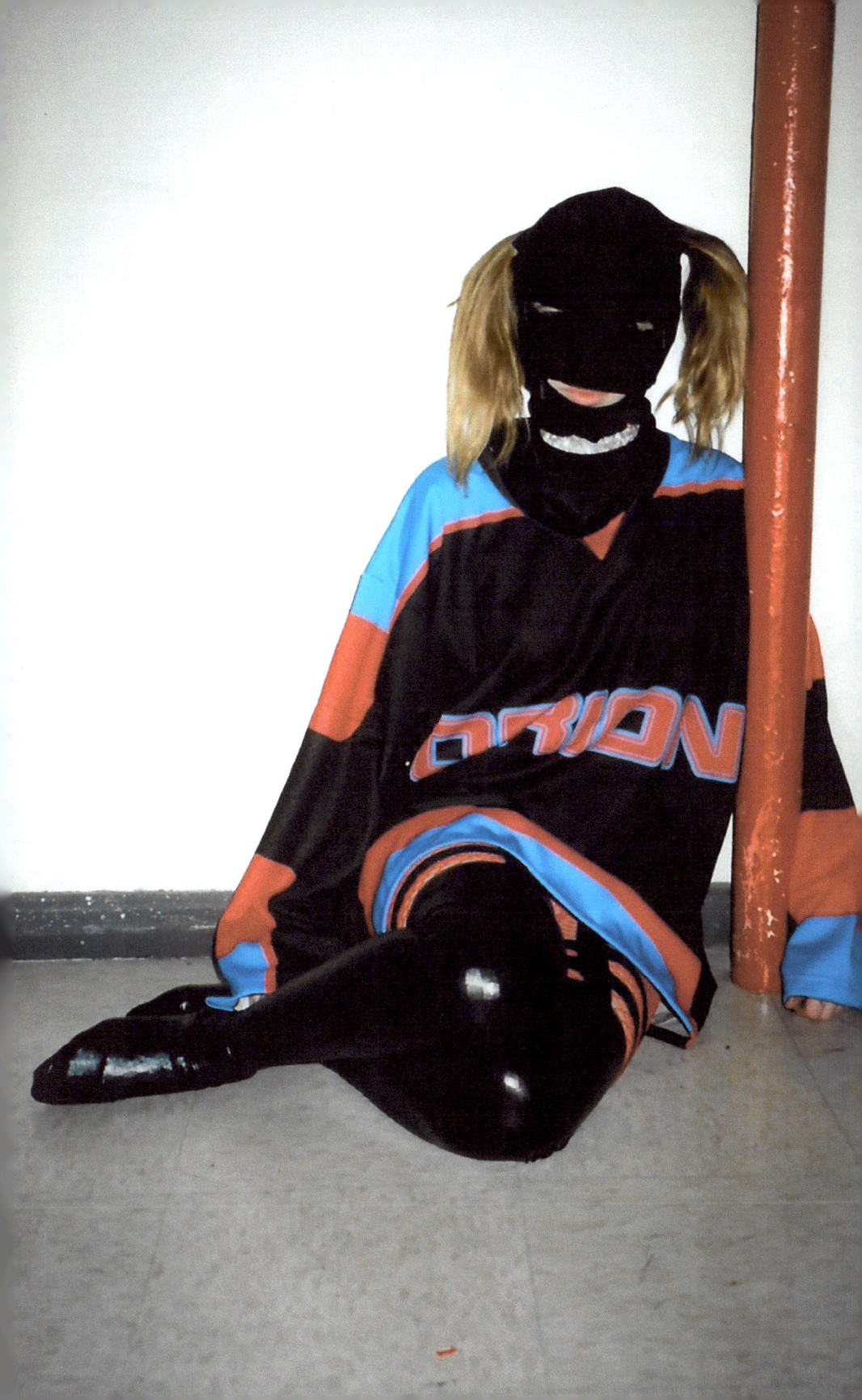

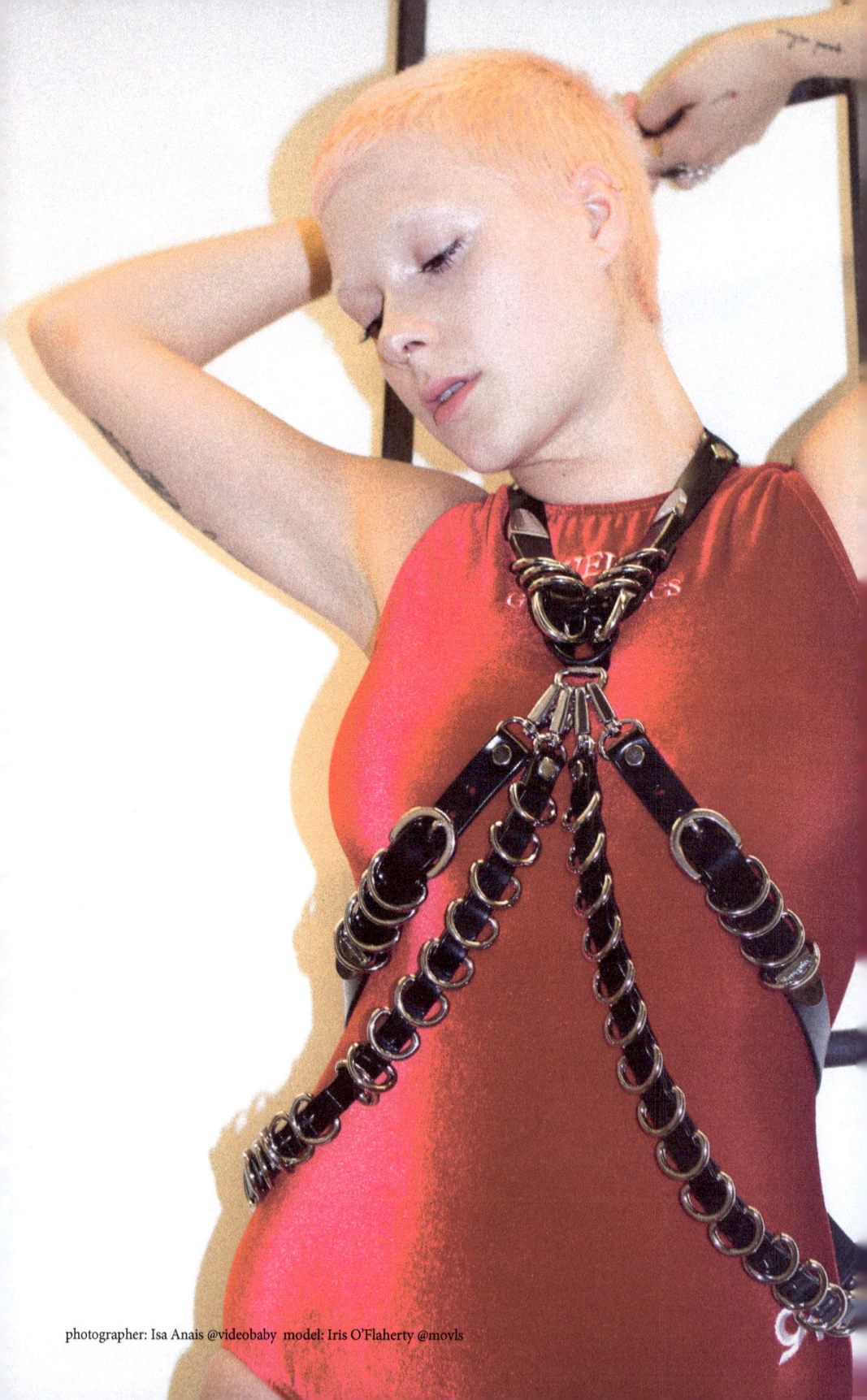

photographer: Isa Anais @videobaby model: Iris O'Flaherty @movls

illustrator: Niamh Donnelly @niamhlabeij

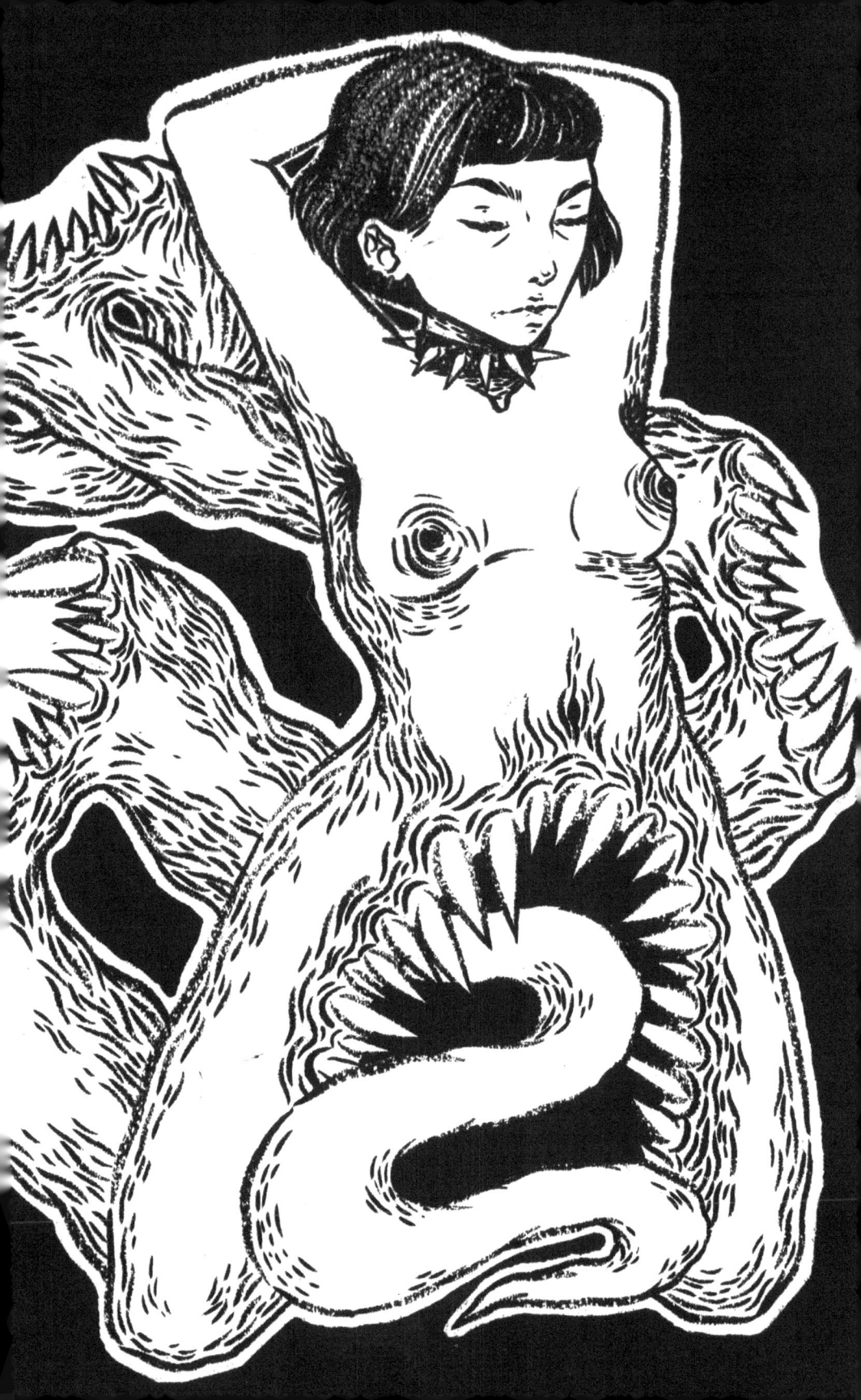

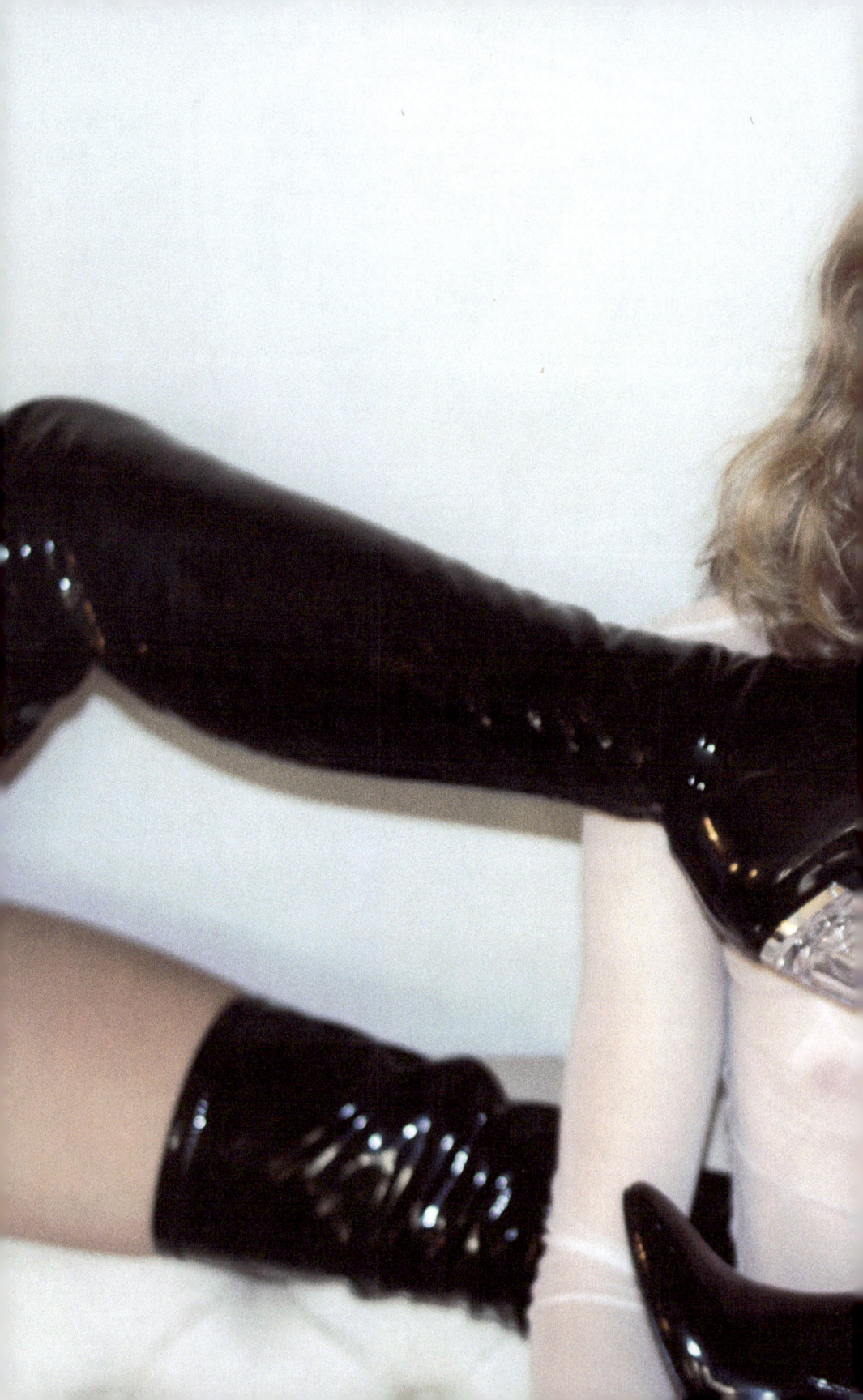

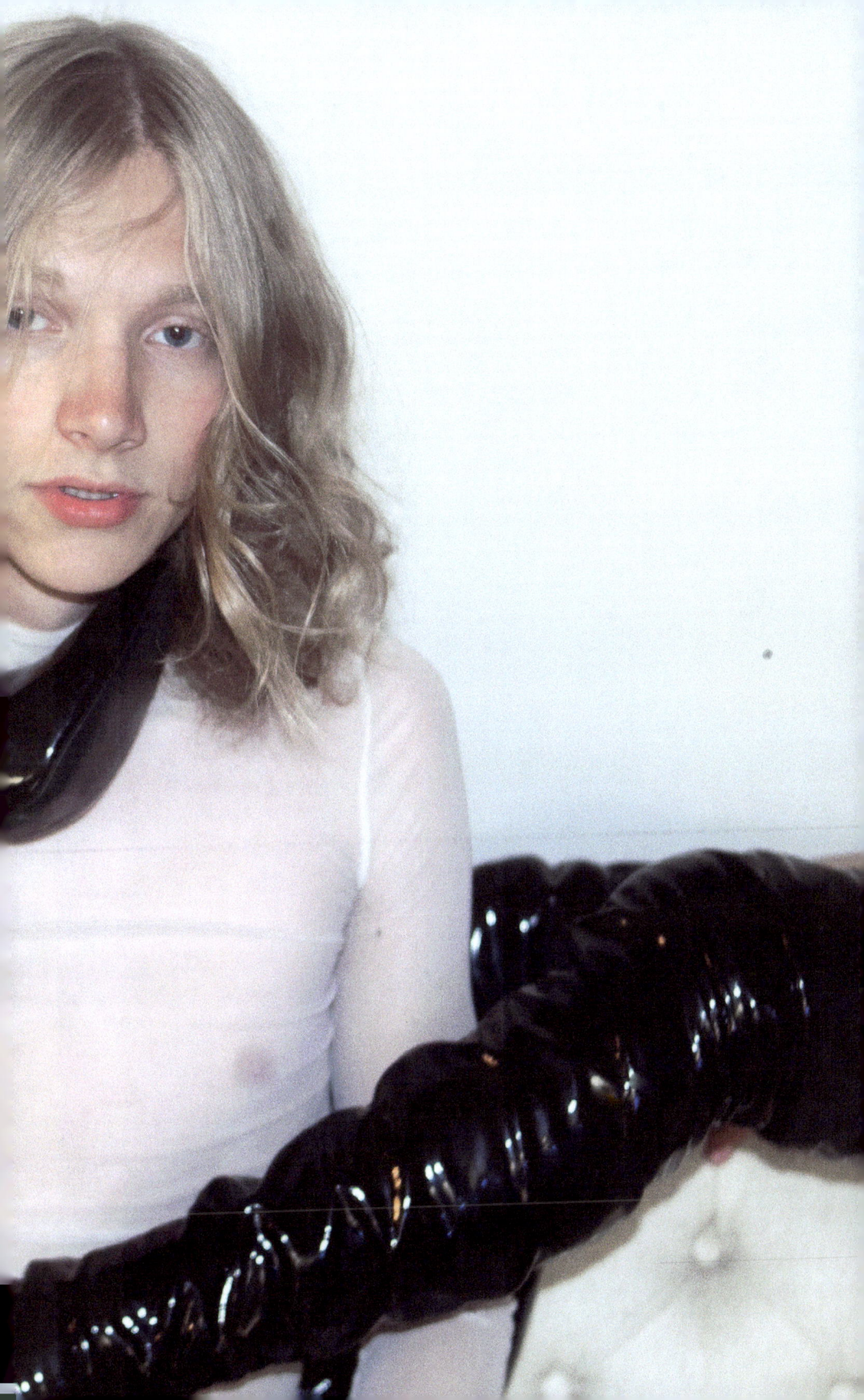

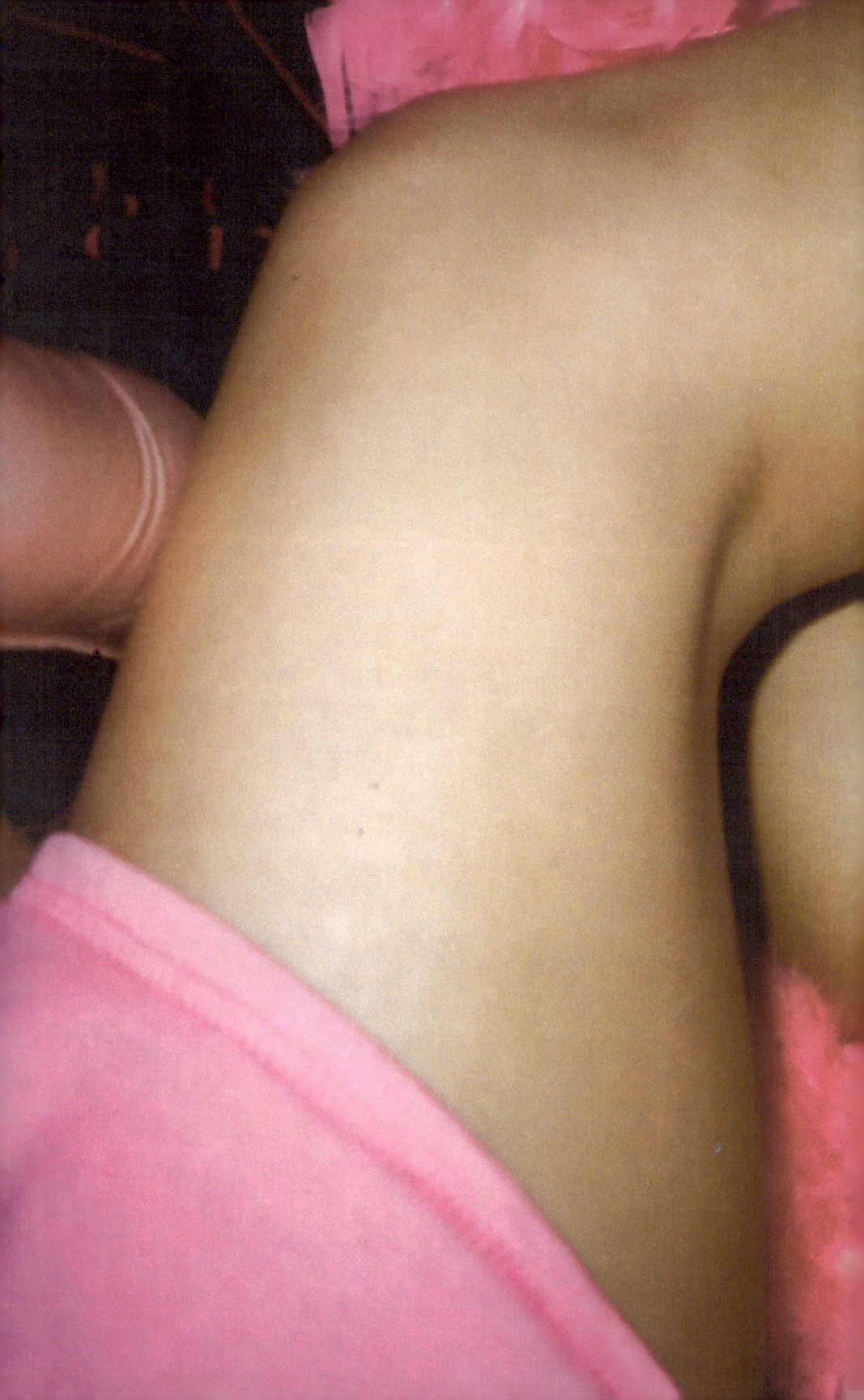

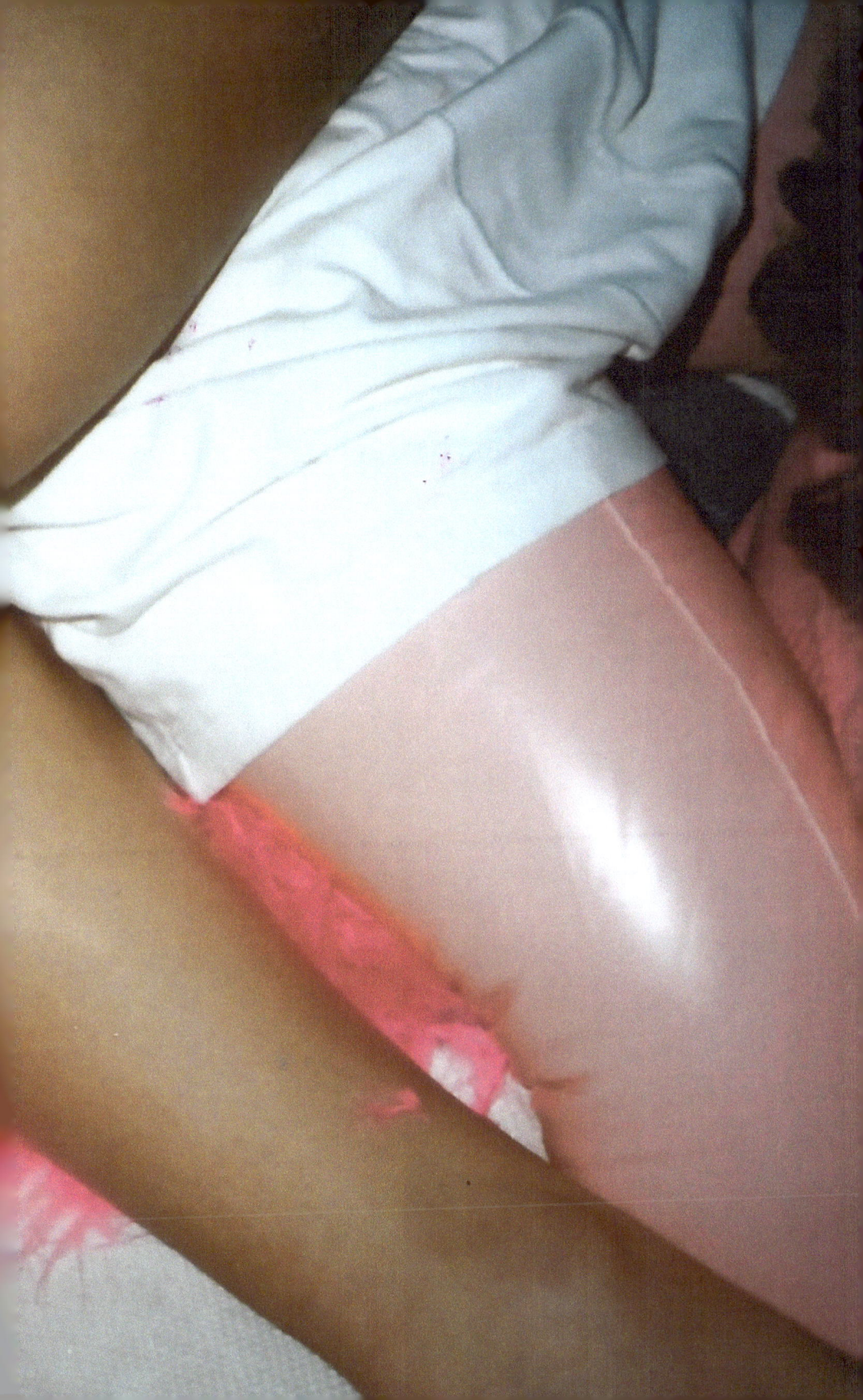

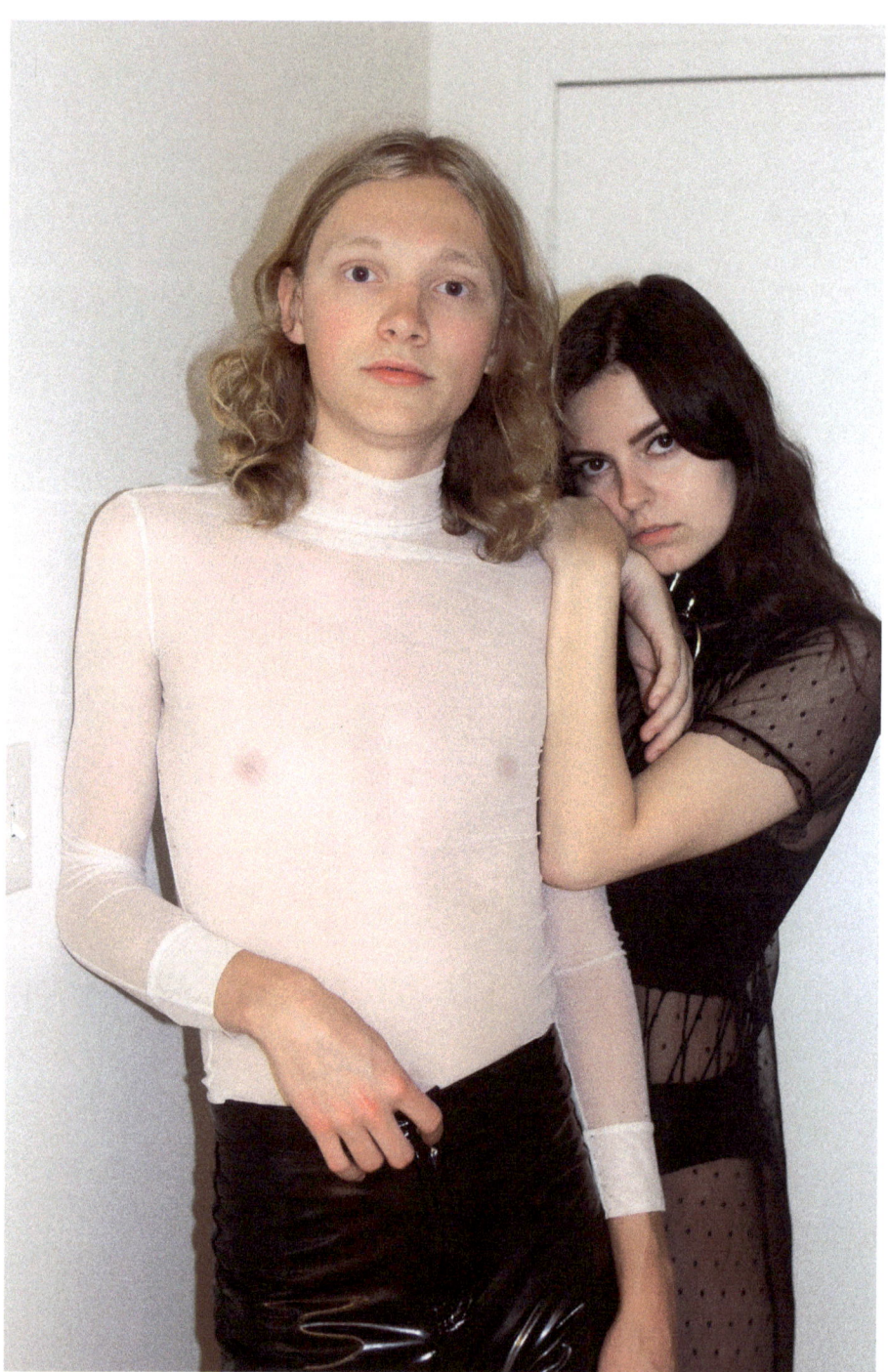

photographer: Isa Anais @videobaby models: Anders Johnson @anderbearjohnson Sami Claire @sami.claire

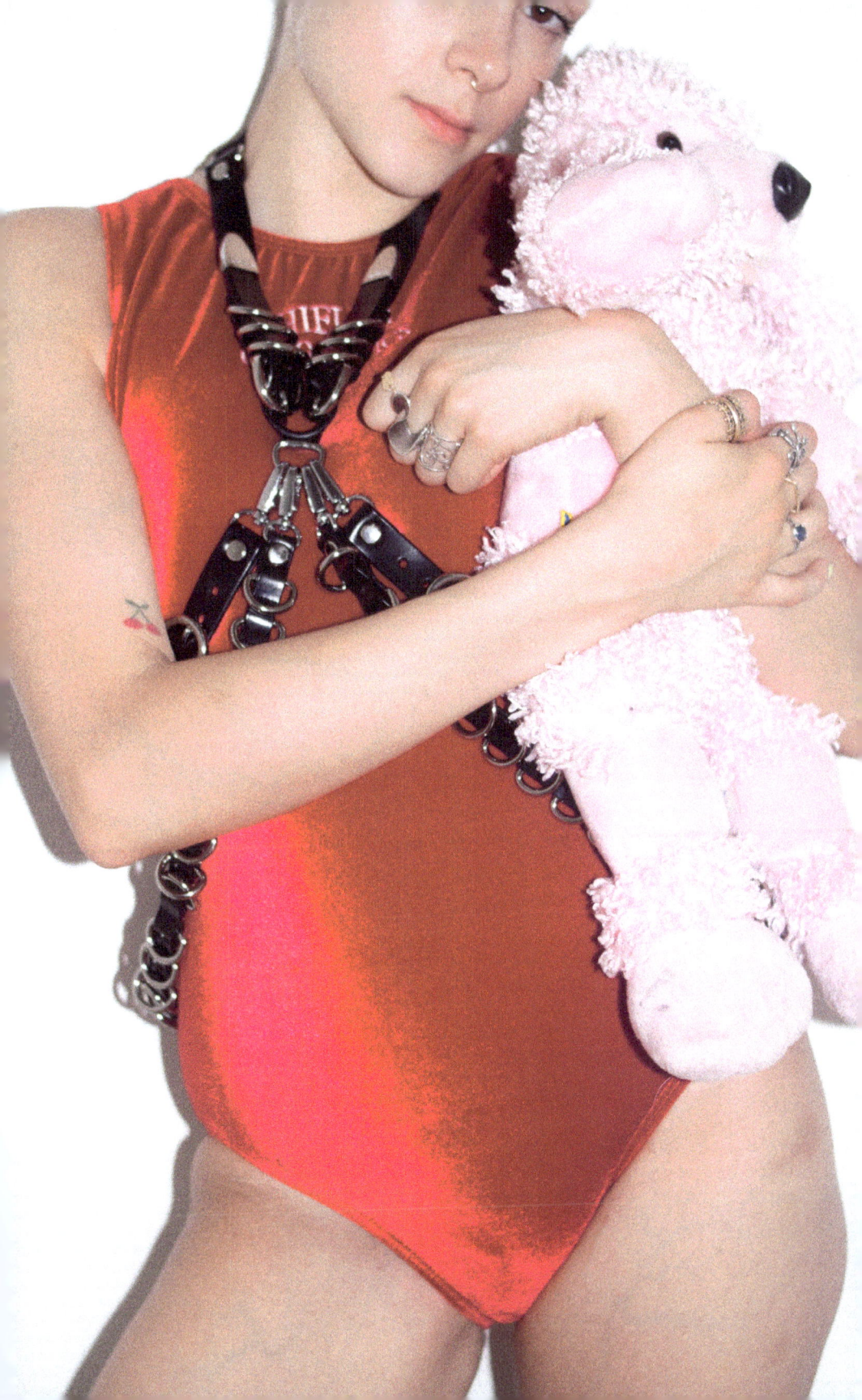

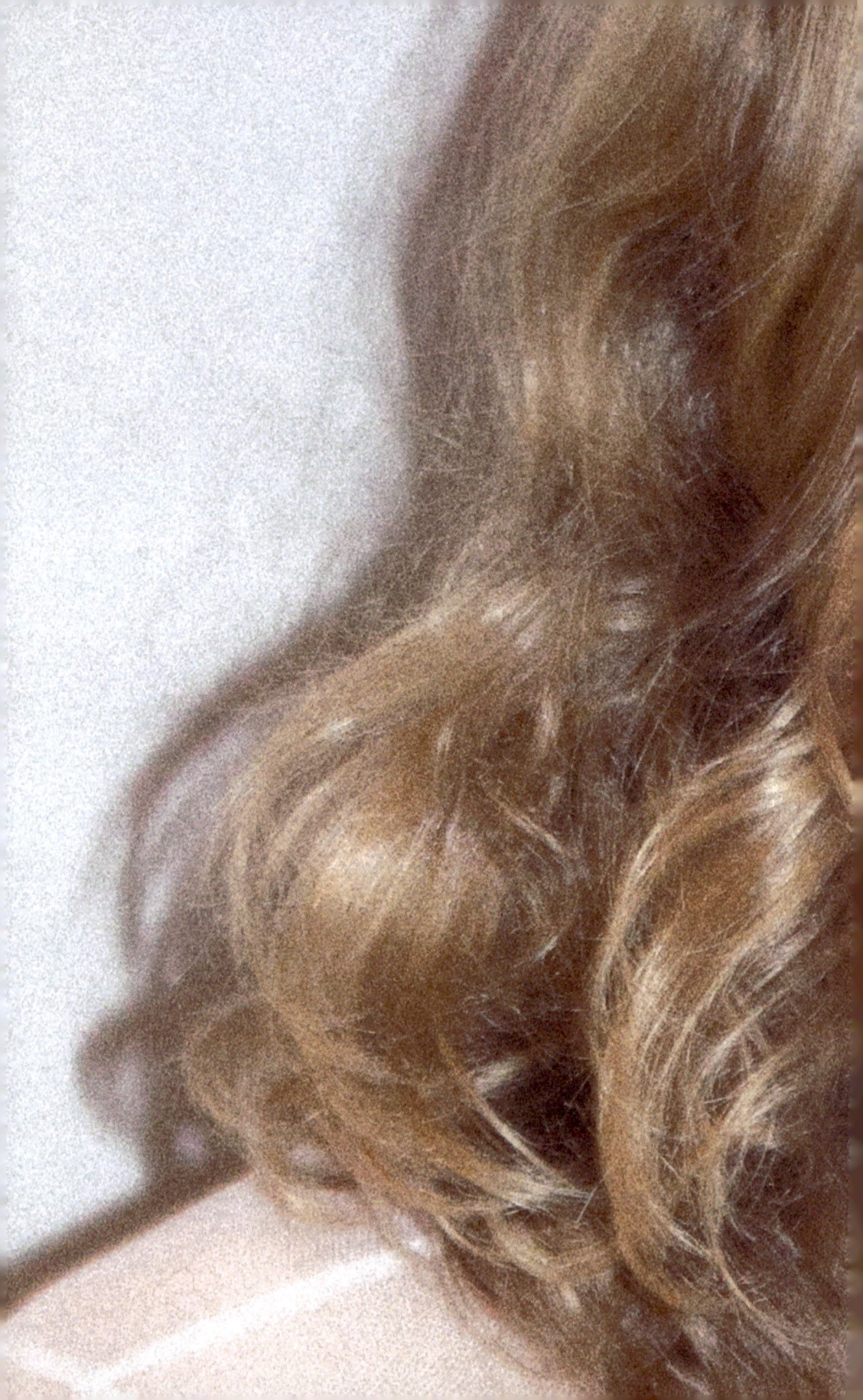

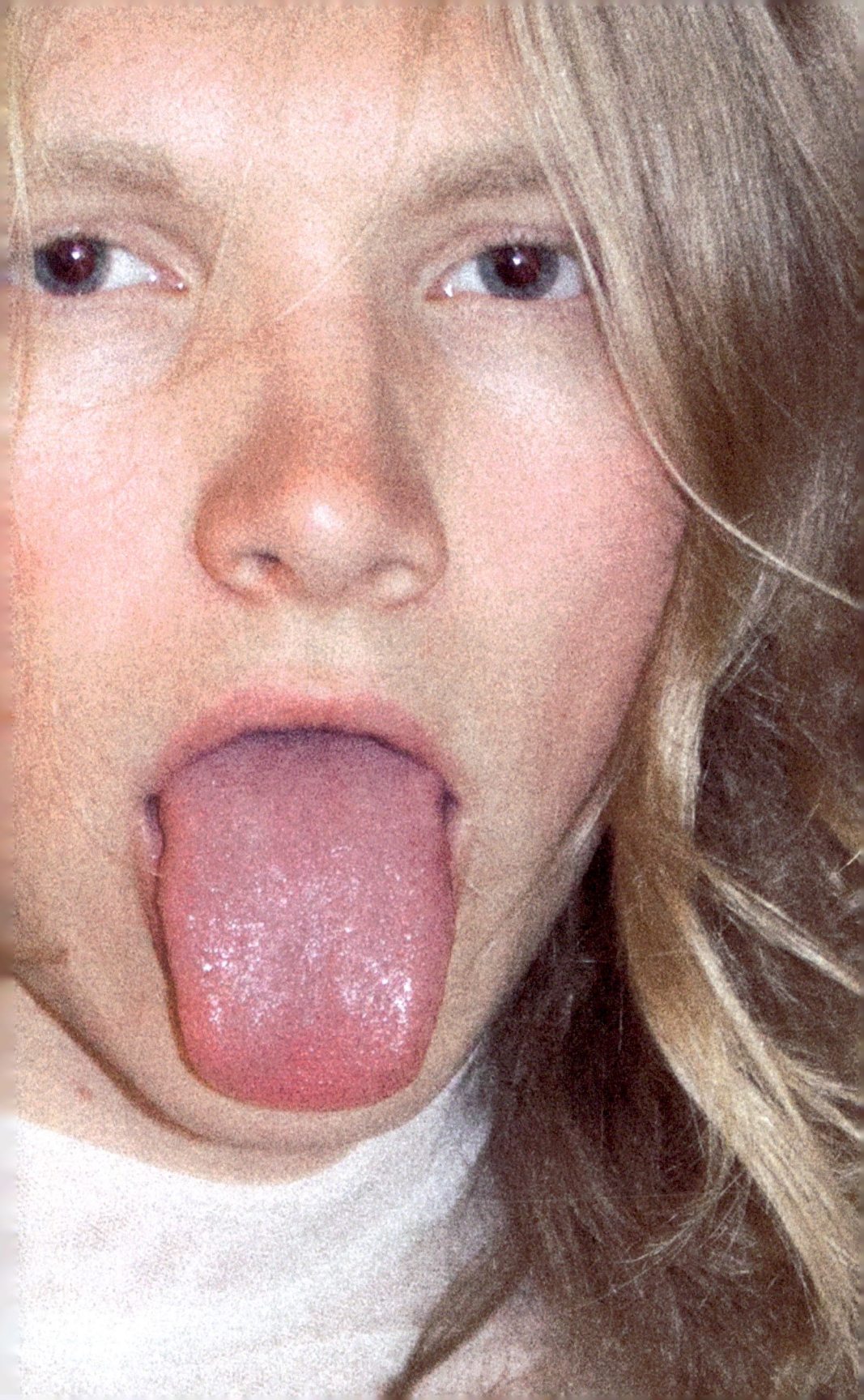

photographer: Orion Connor @orion.process

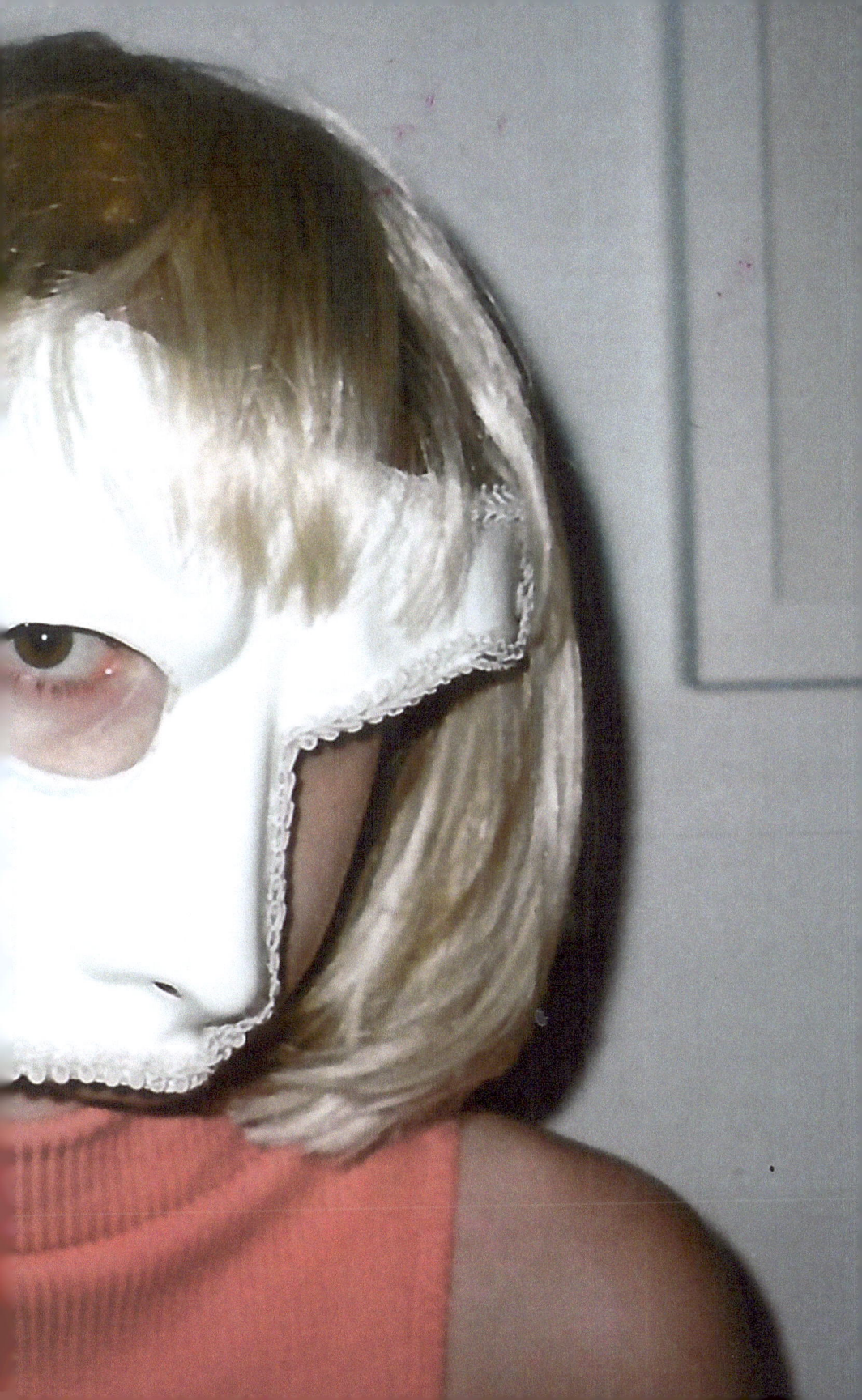

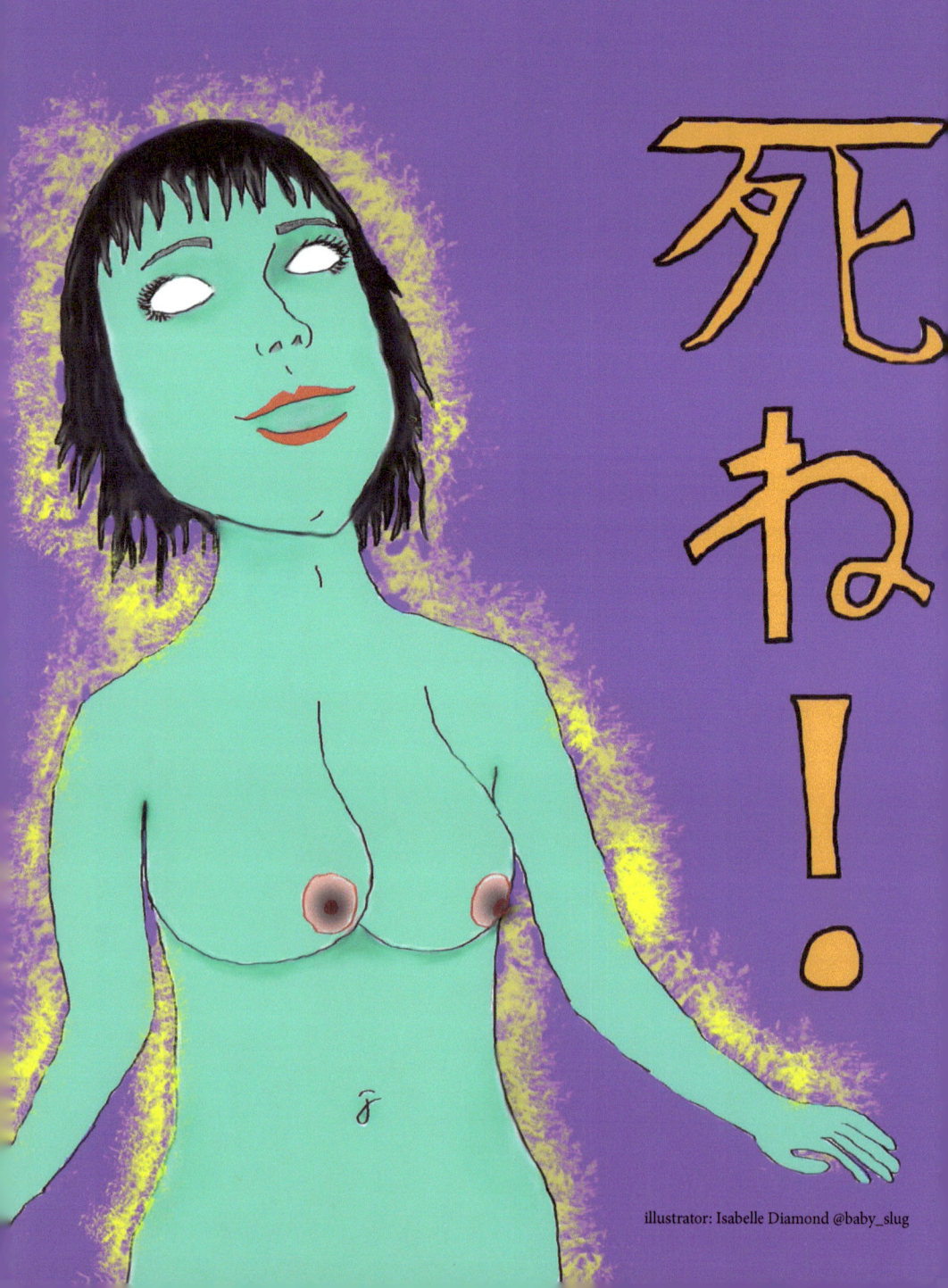

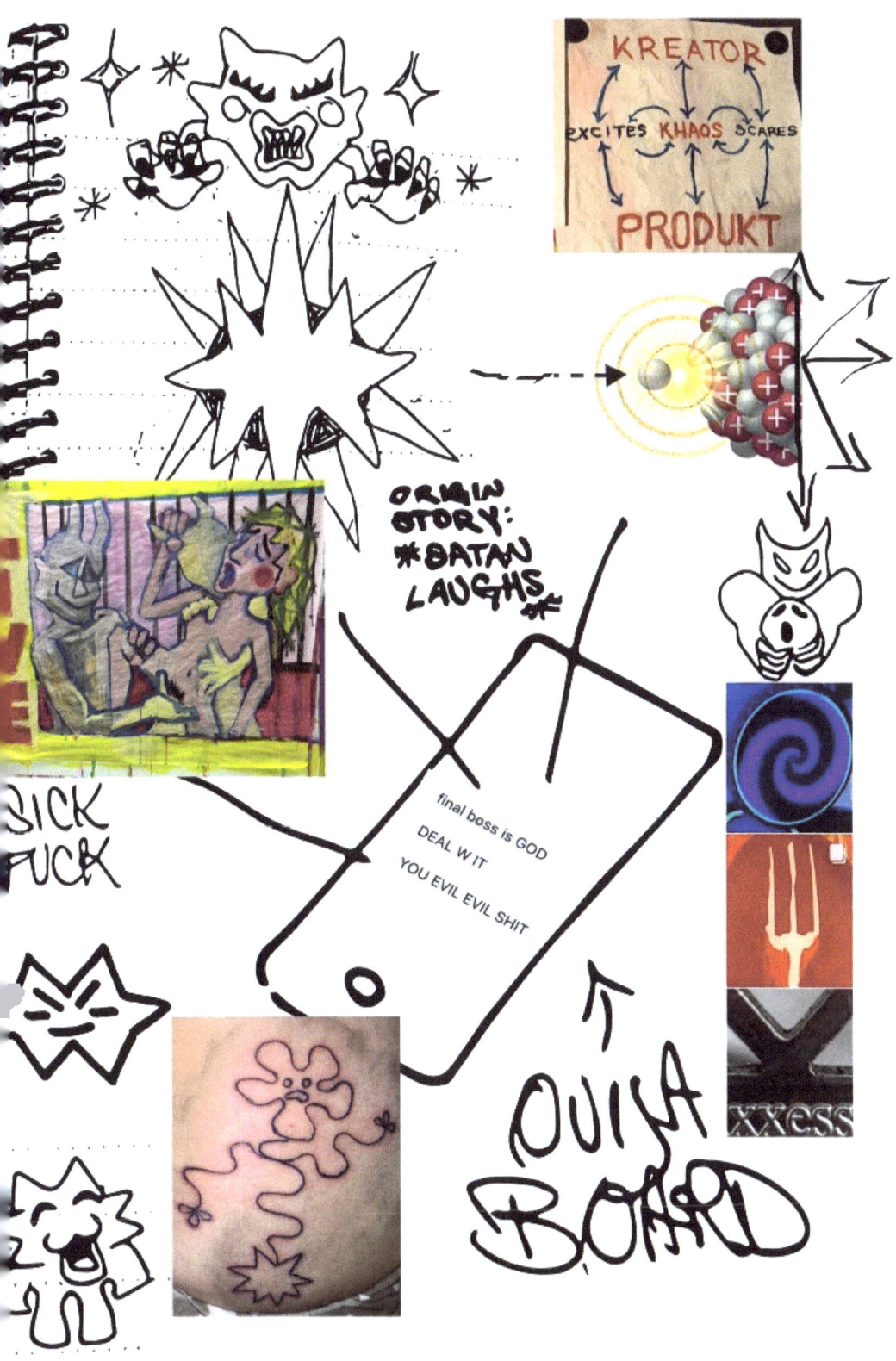

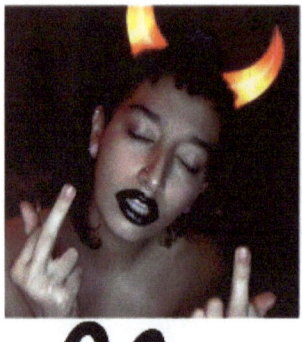

sleeping god,
is there a point in questioning the game
is there a point in questioning the game
is there a point in questioning the game
is there a point in questioning the game
is there a point in questioning the game

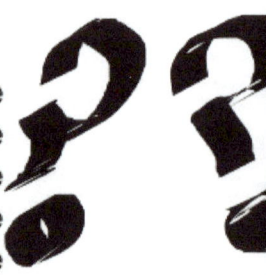

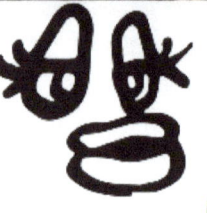

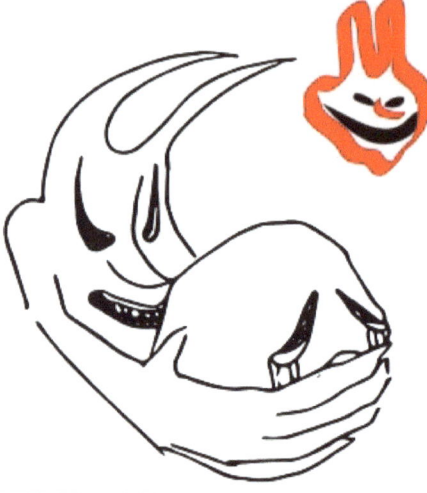

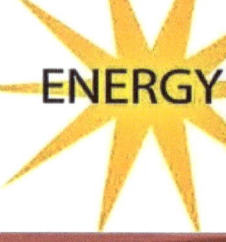 ENERGY

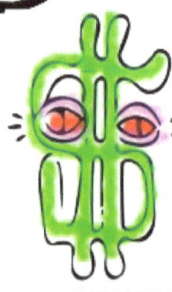

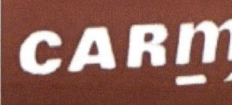

MWAHAHAHAHAHA

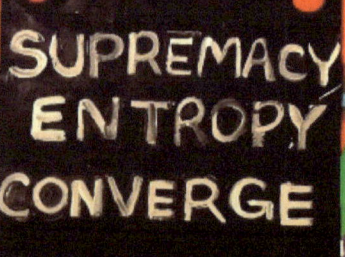

SUPREMACY
ENTROPY
CONVERGE

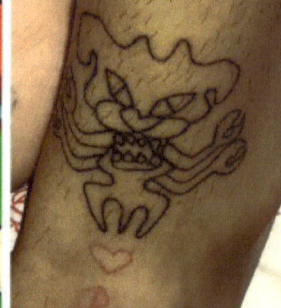

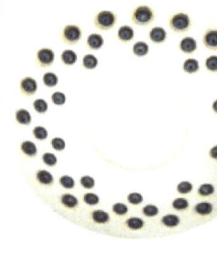

10 REASONS
YOUR PRAYERS
AREN'T BEING
ANSWERED

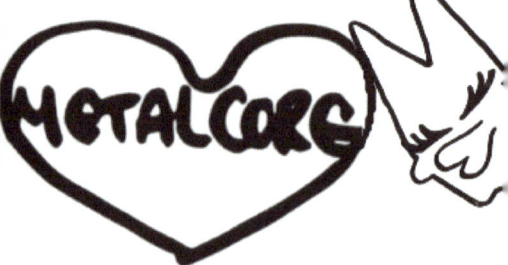

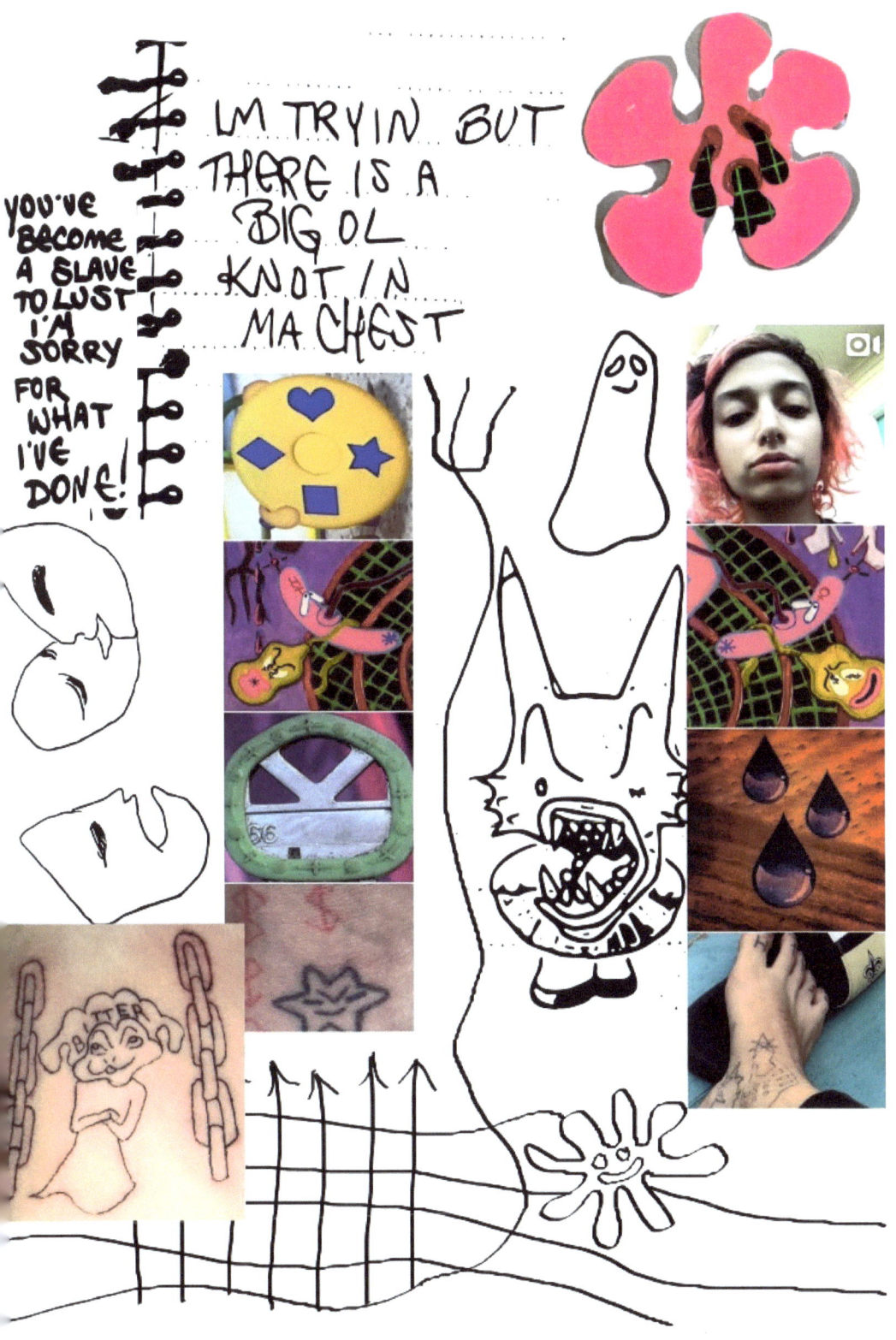

illustrator: @smut_kingdom

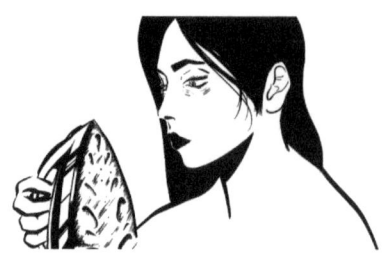

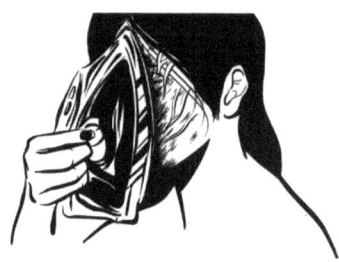

I DON'T
FEEL COMFORTABLE

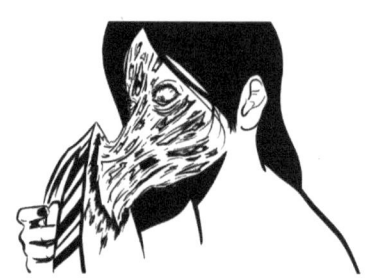

IN MY
OWN SKIN...

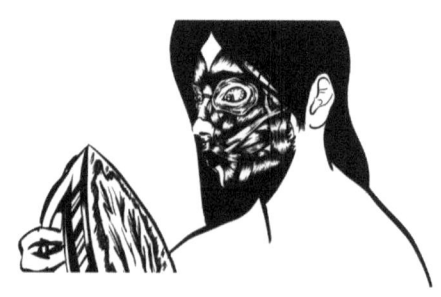

illustrator: @thehopelessartist

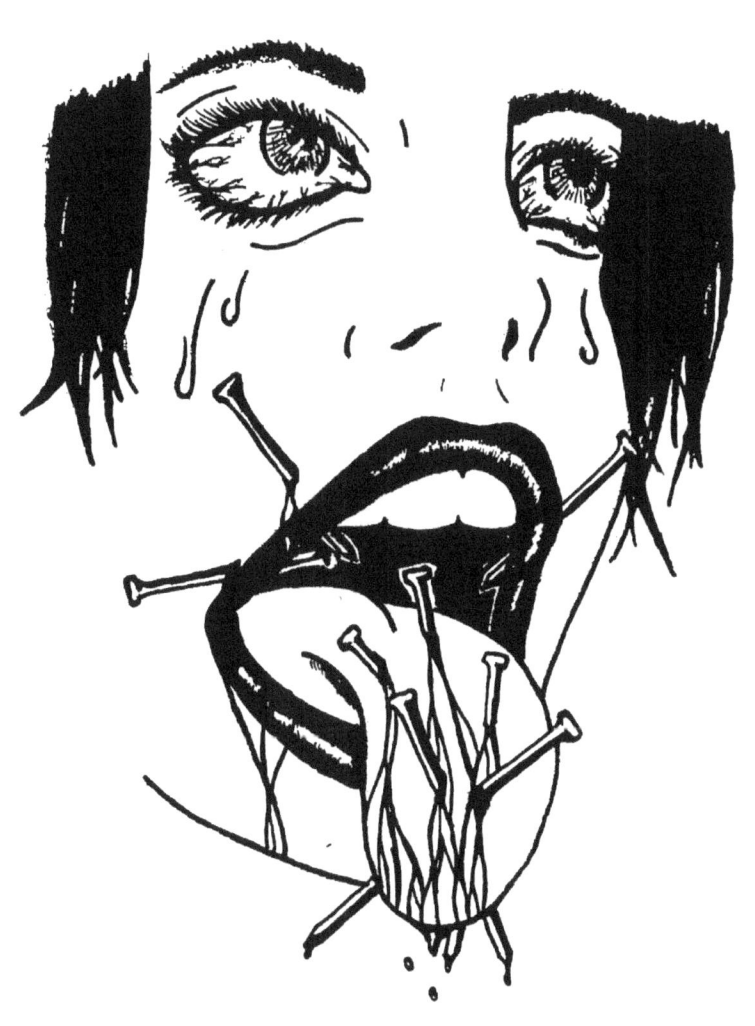

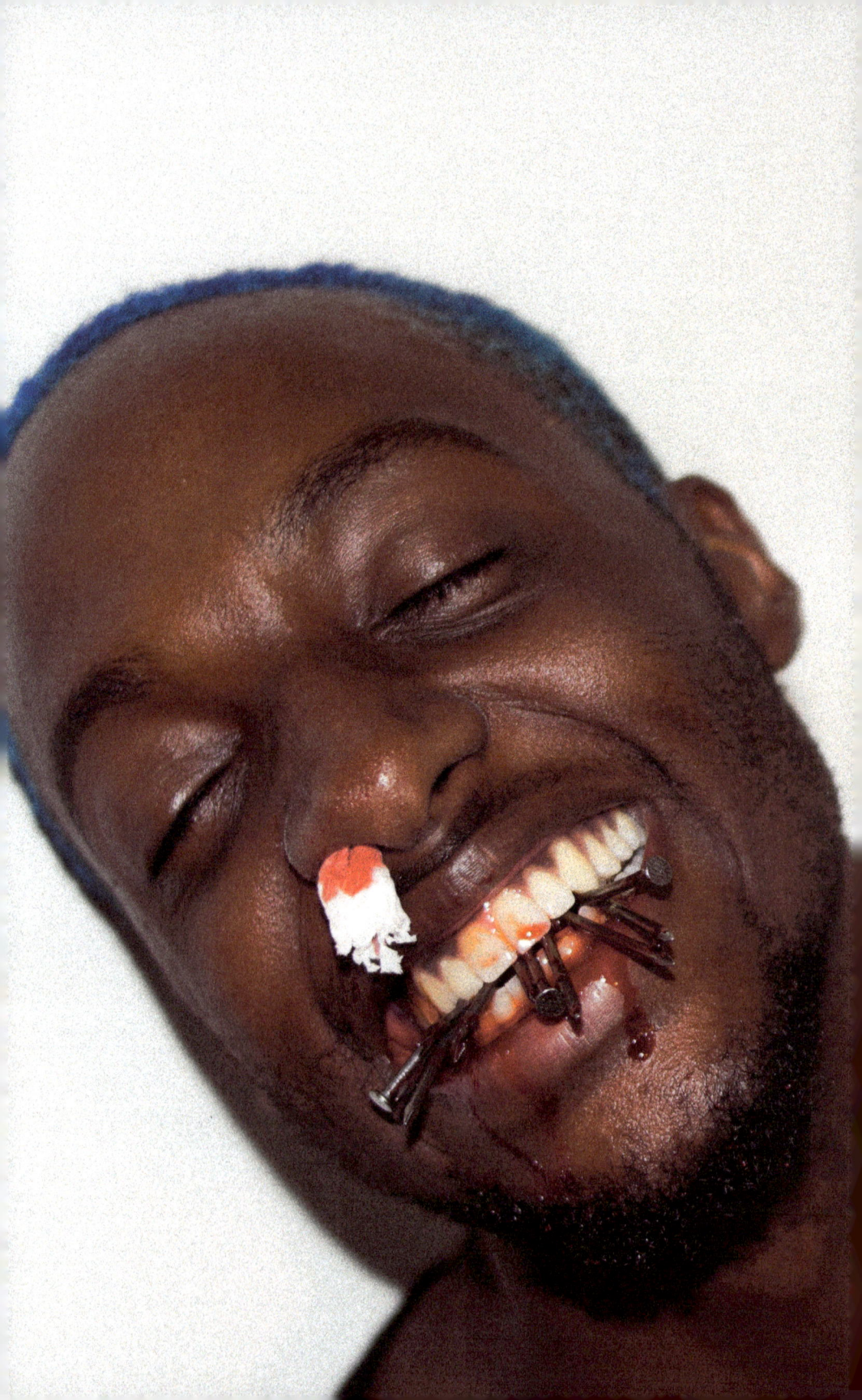

photographer: Isa Anais @videobaby
model: Ehiorobo Igiehon @ehiorobo

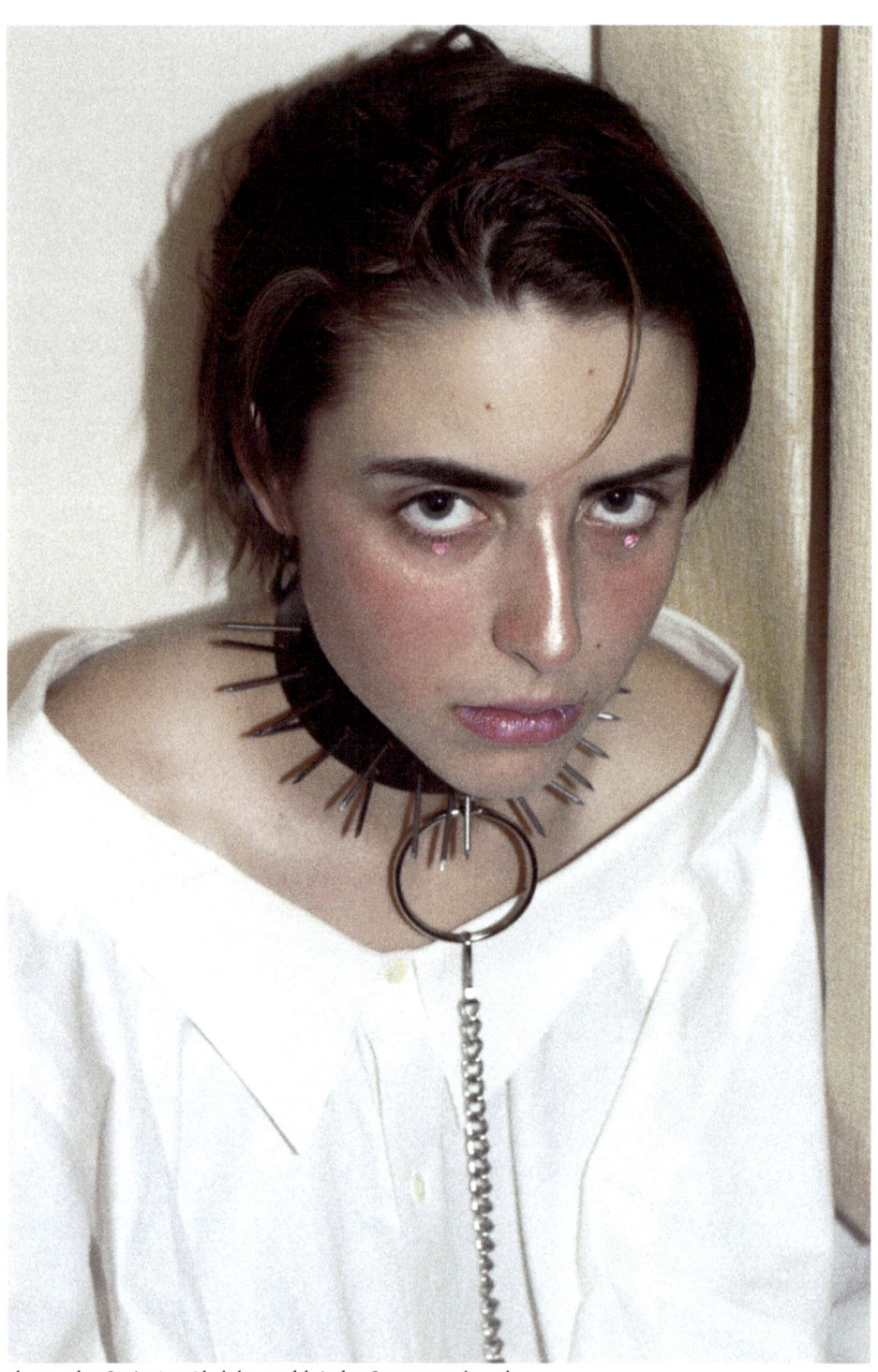

photographer: Isa Anais @videobaby   model: Andrea Stevenson @aka.cacha

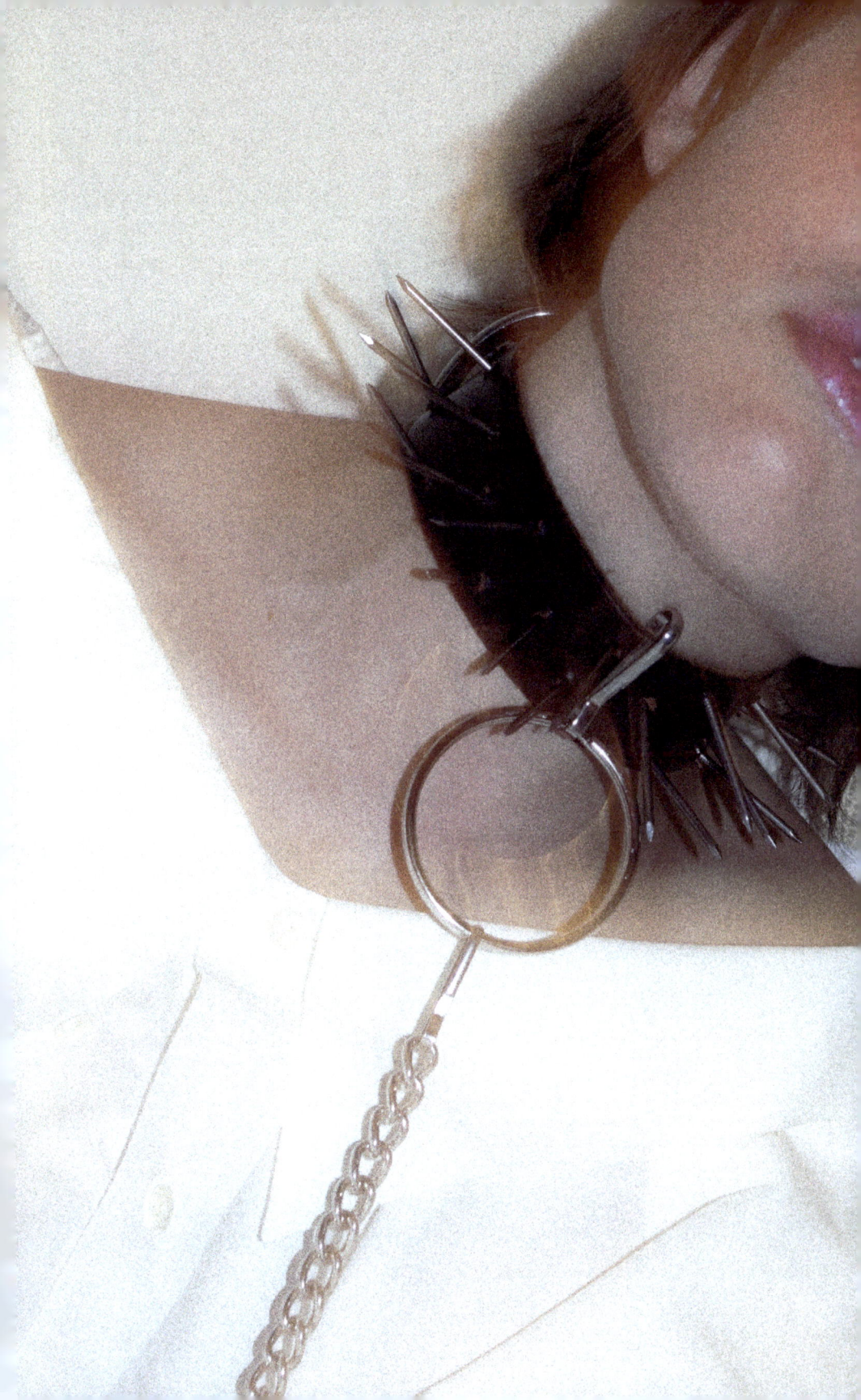

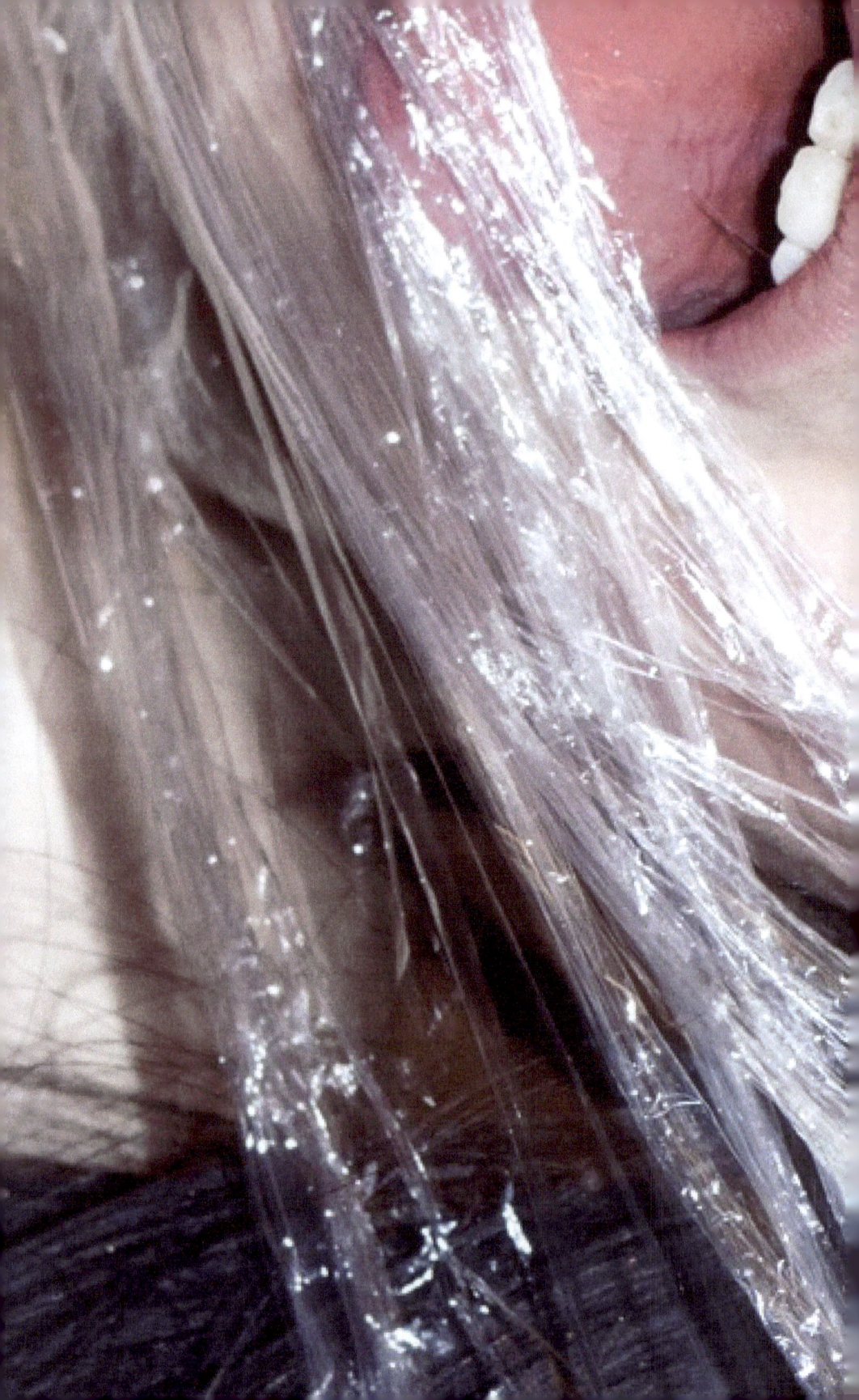

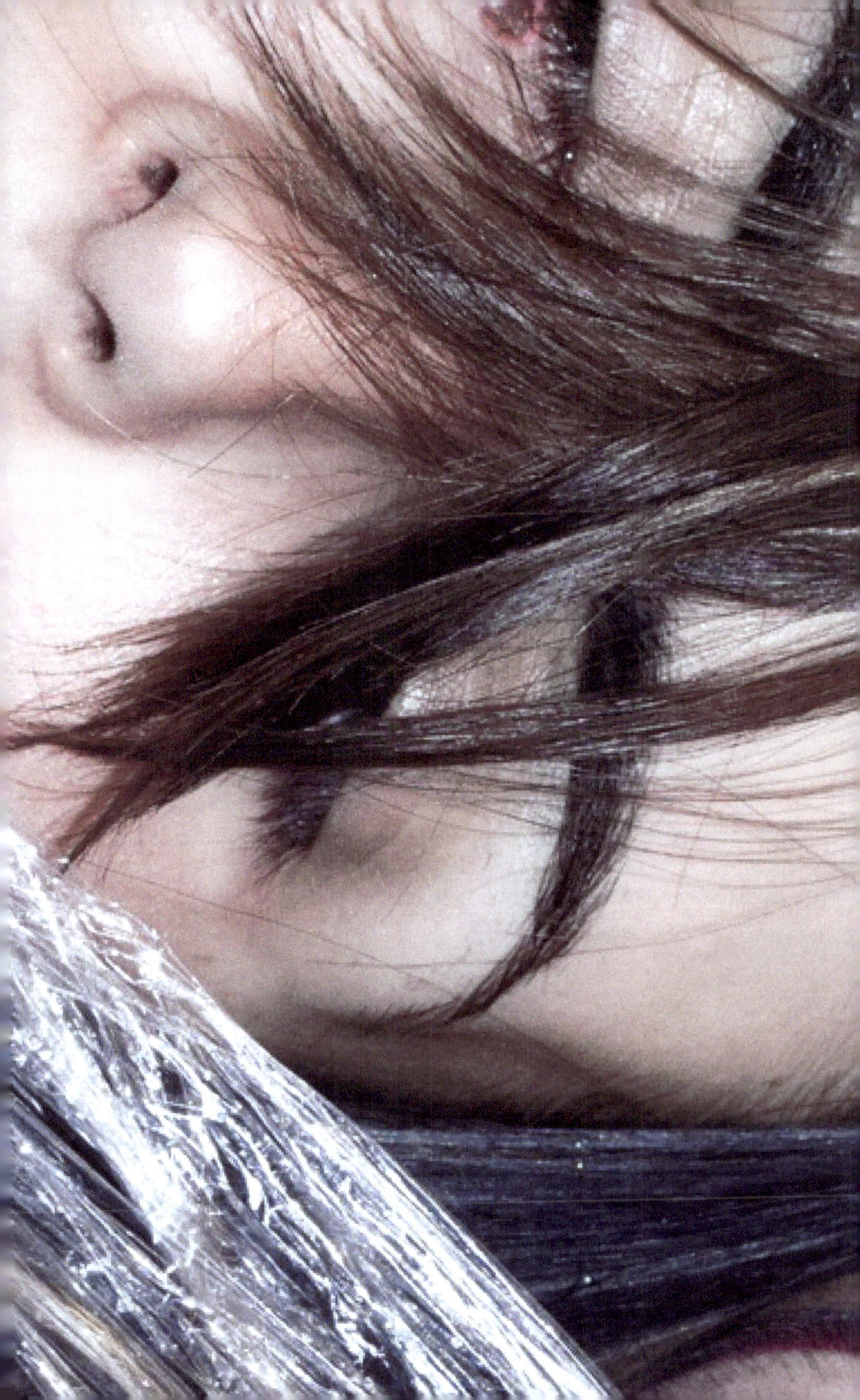

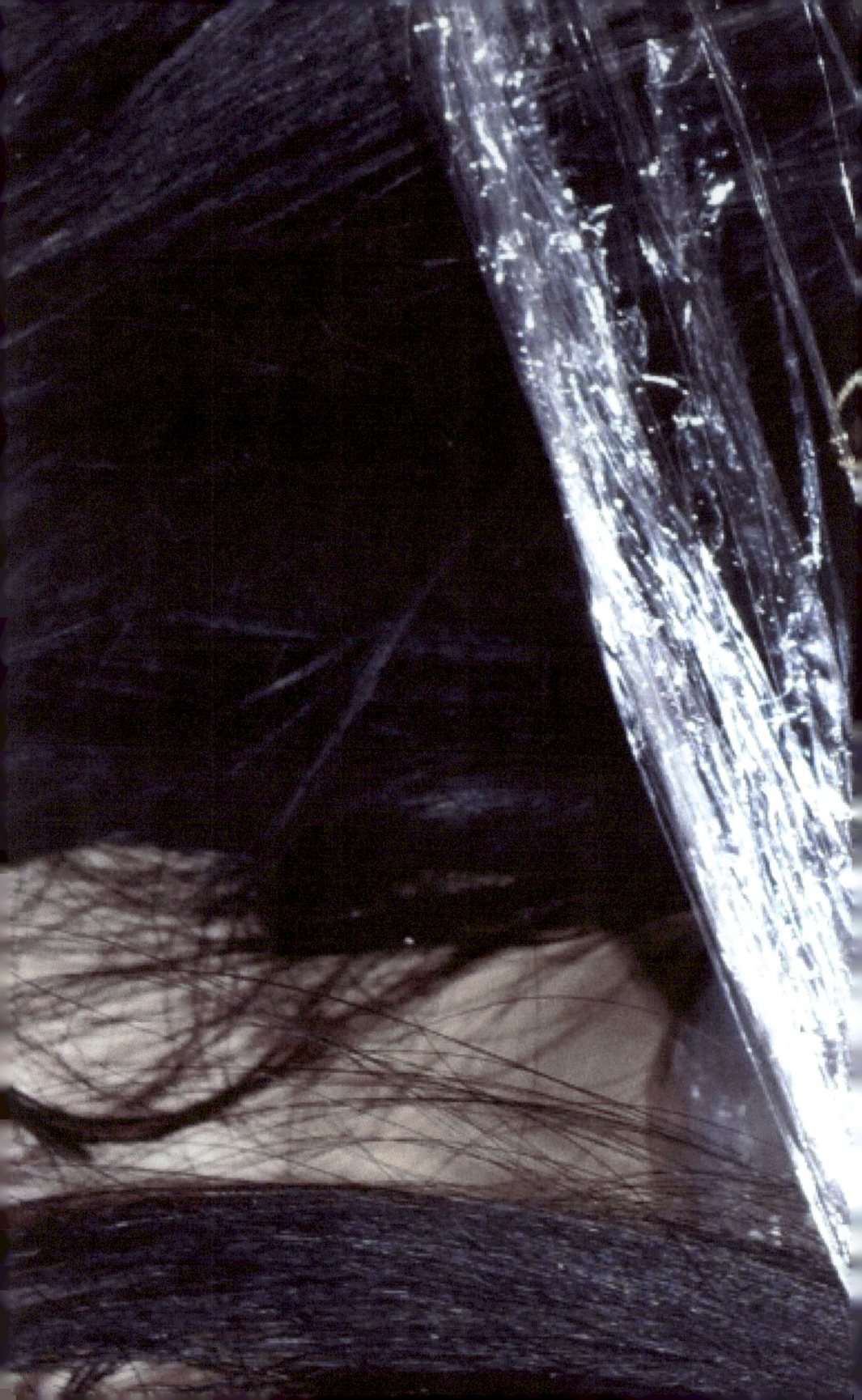

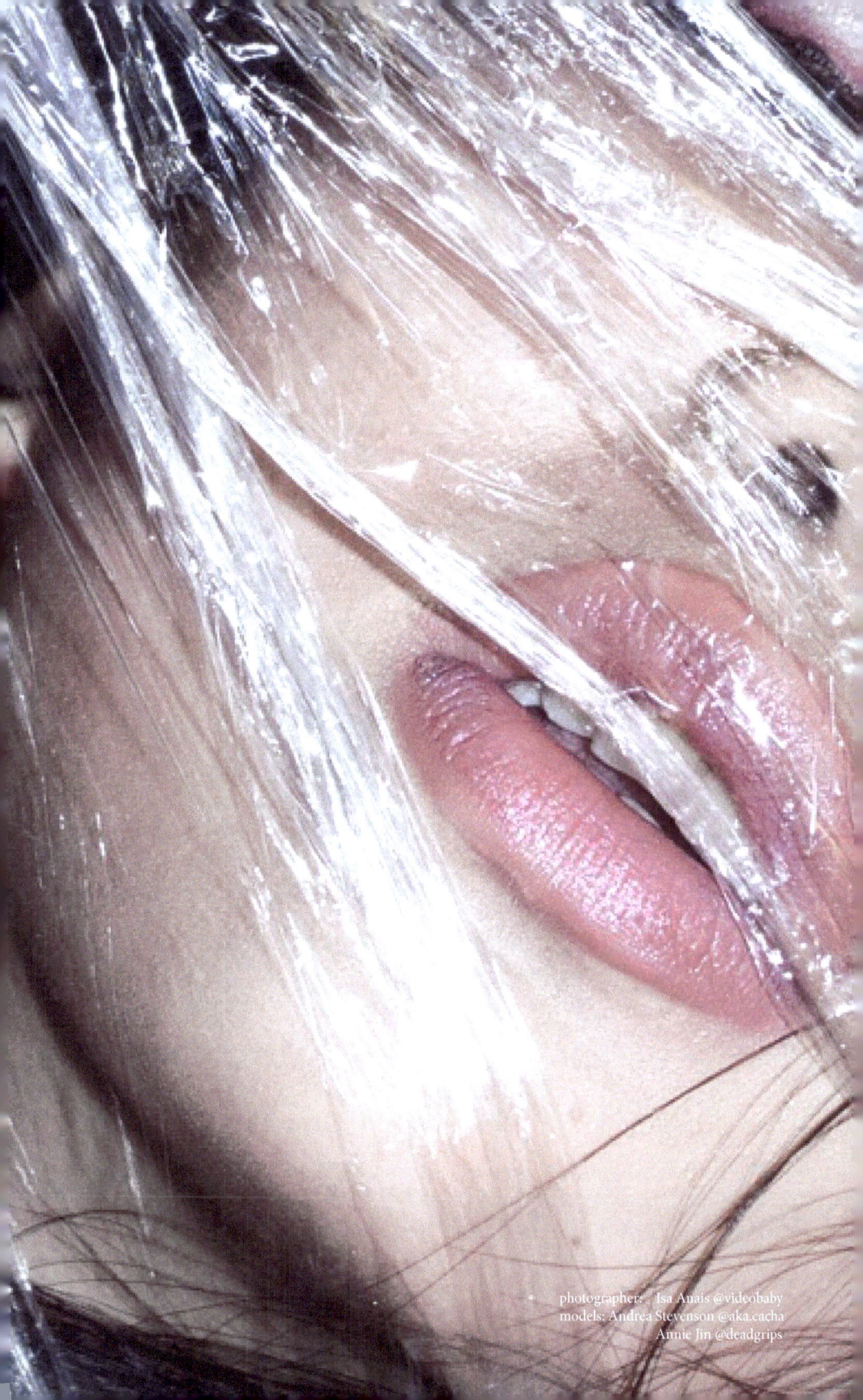

photographers: Isa Anaïs @videobaby
models: Andrea Stevenson @aka.cacha
Annie Jin @deadgrips

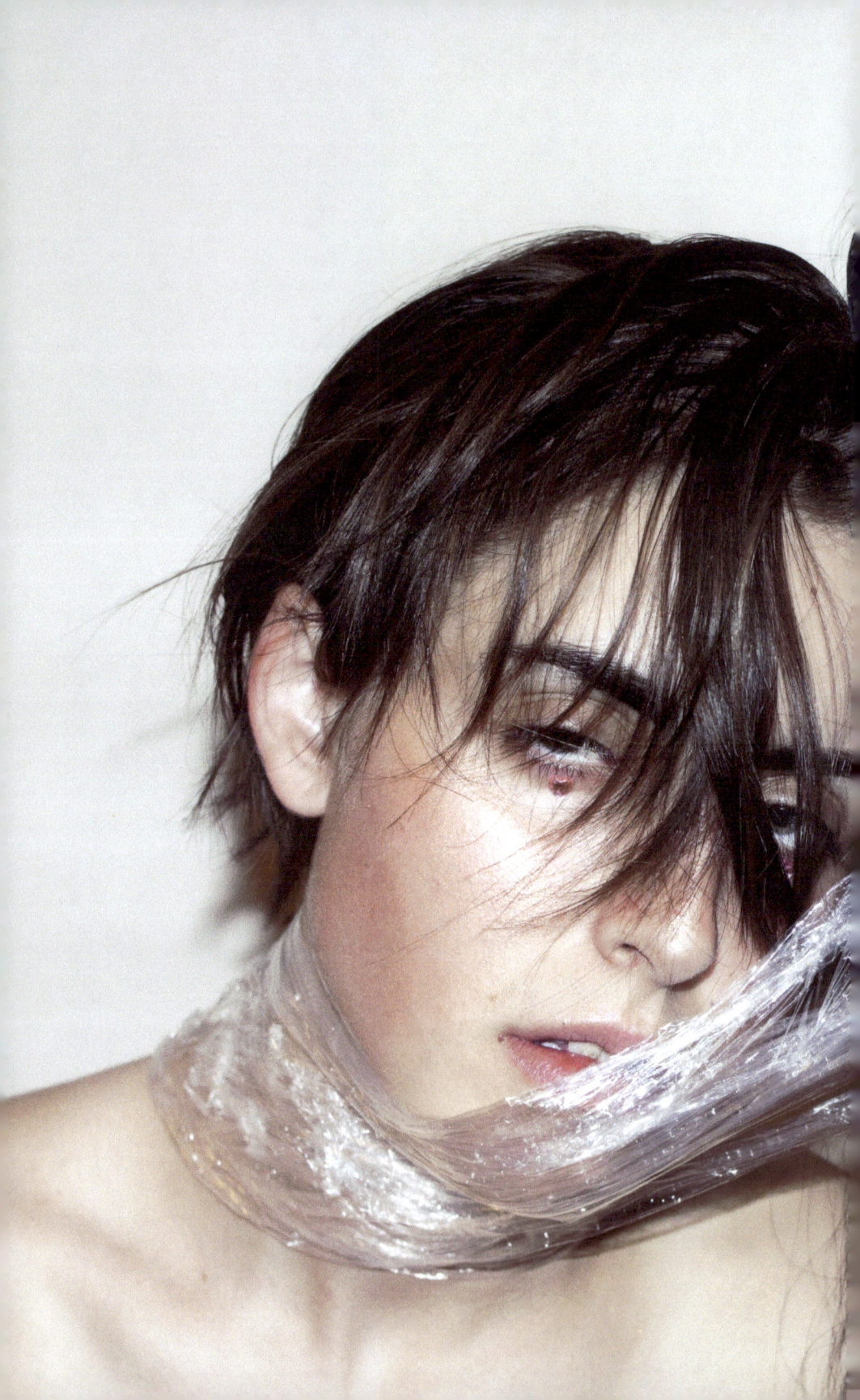

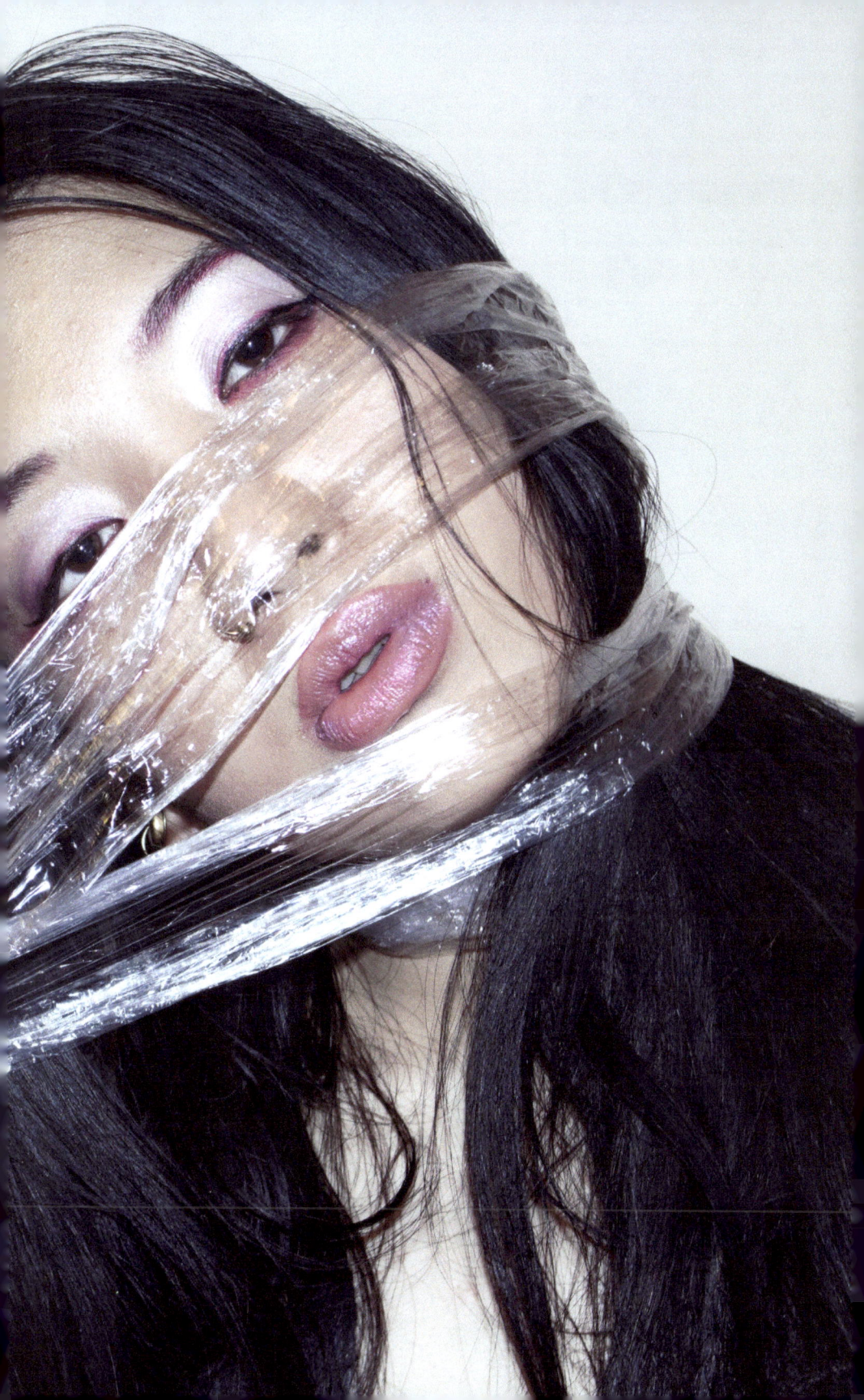

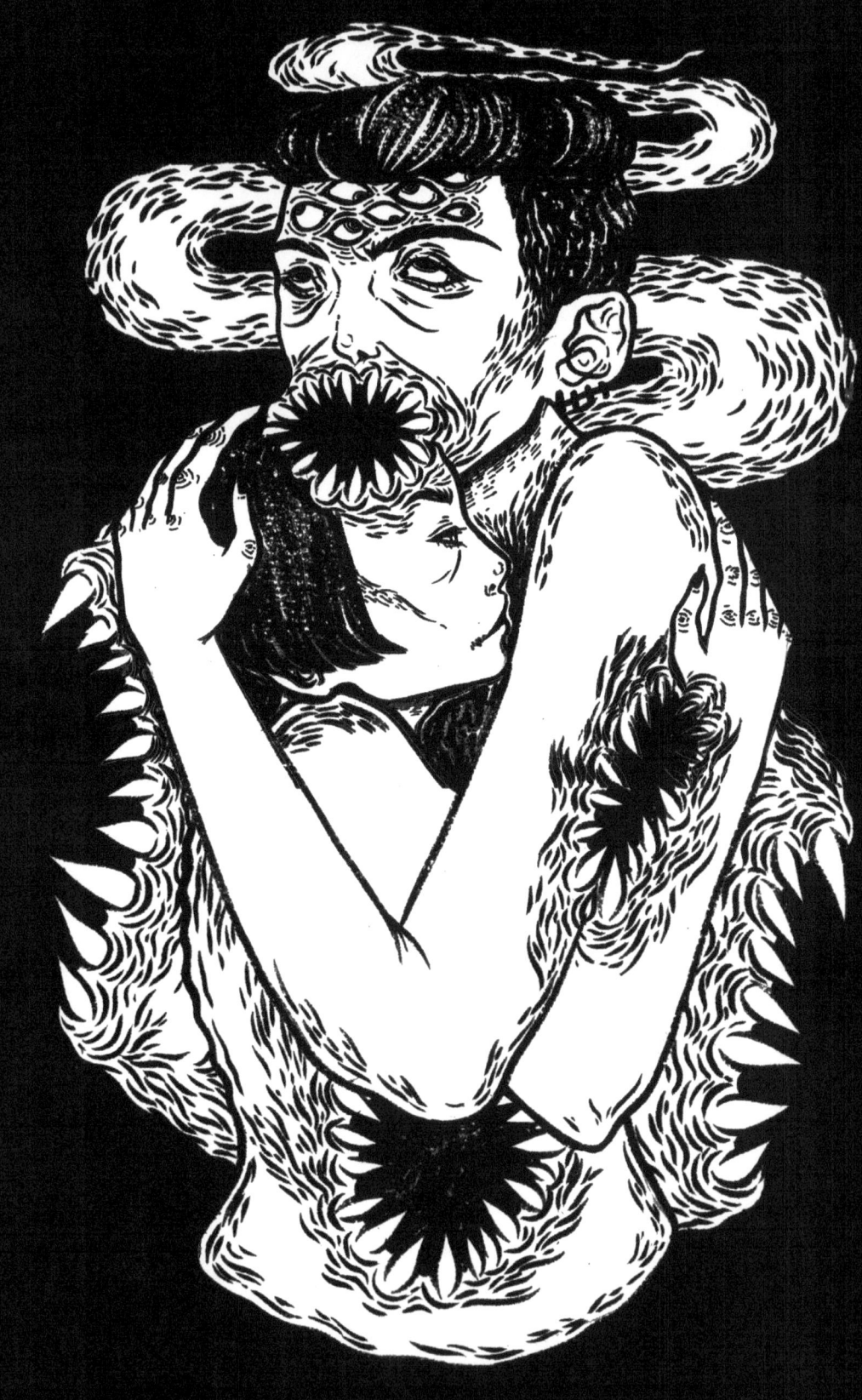

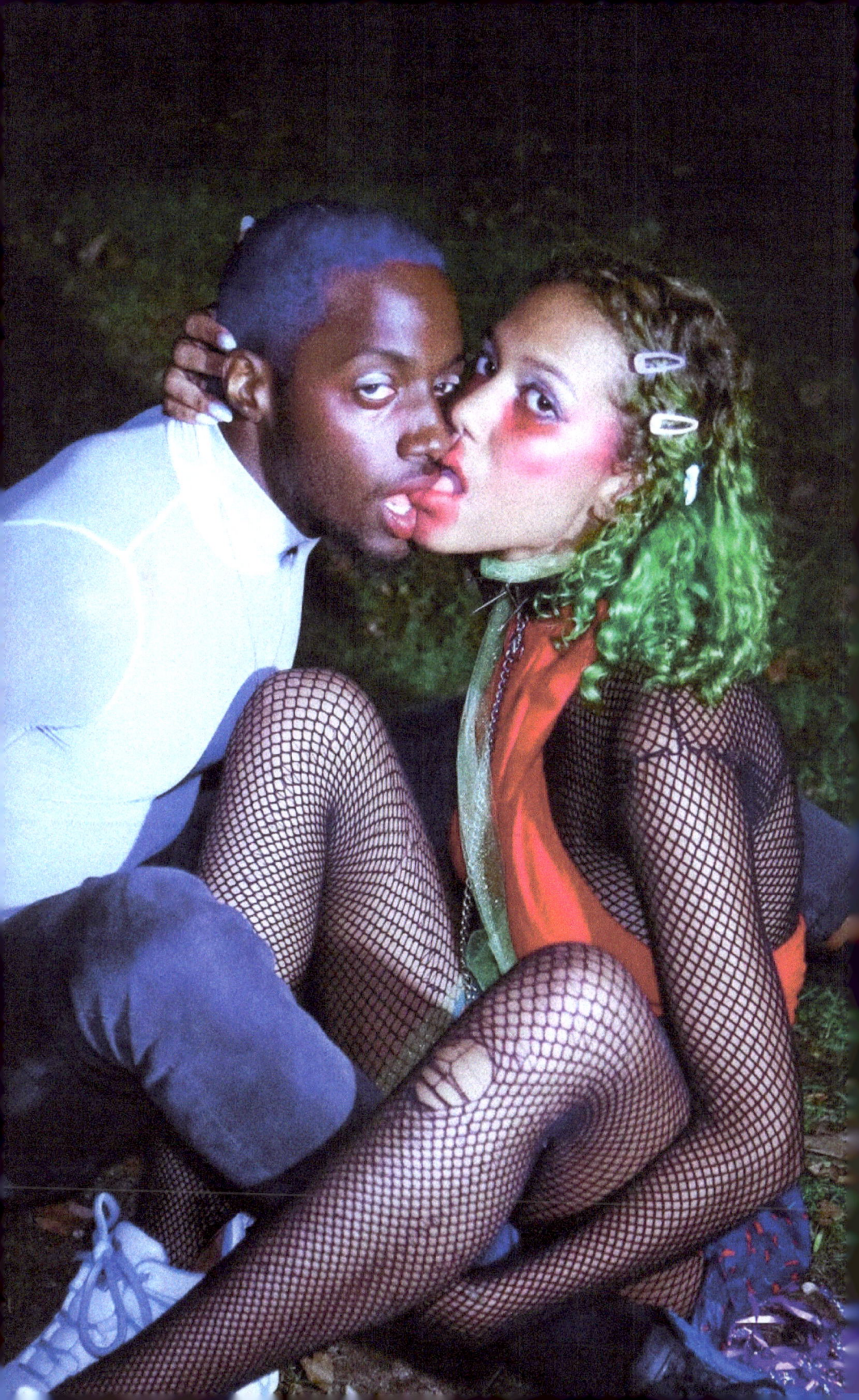

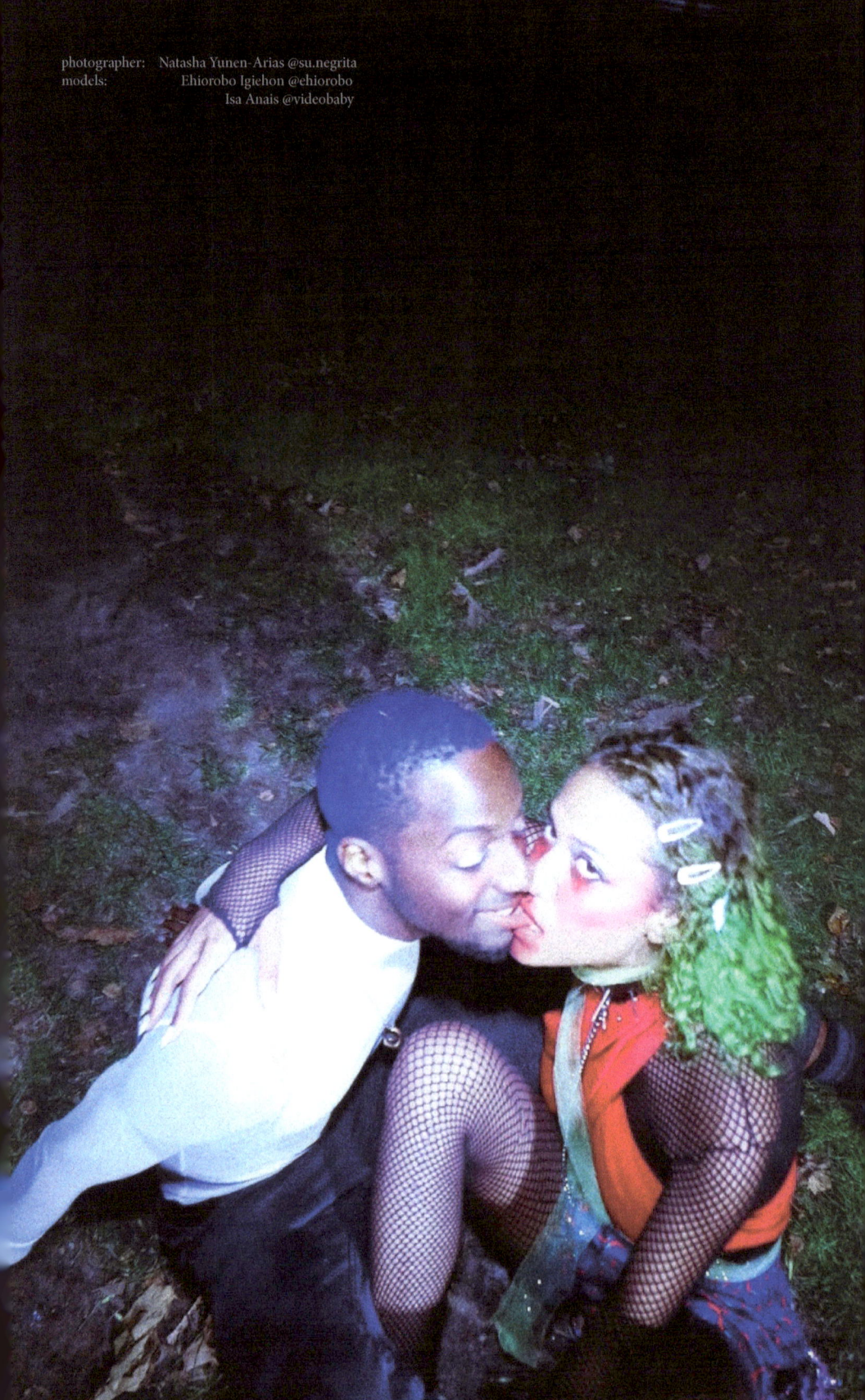

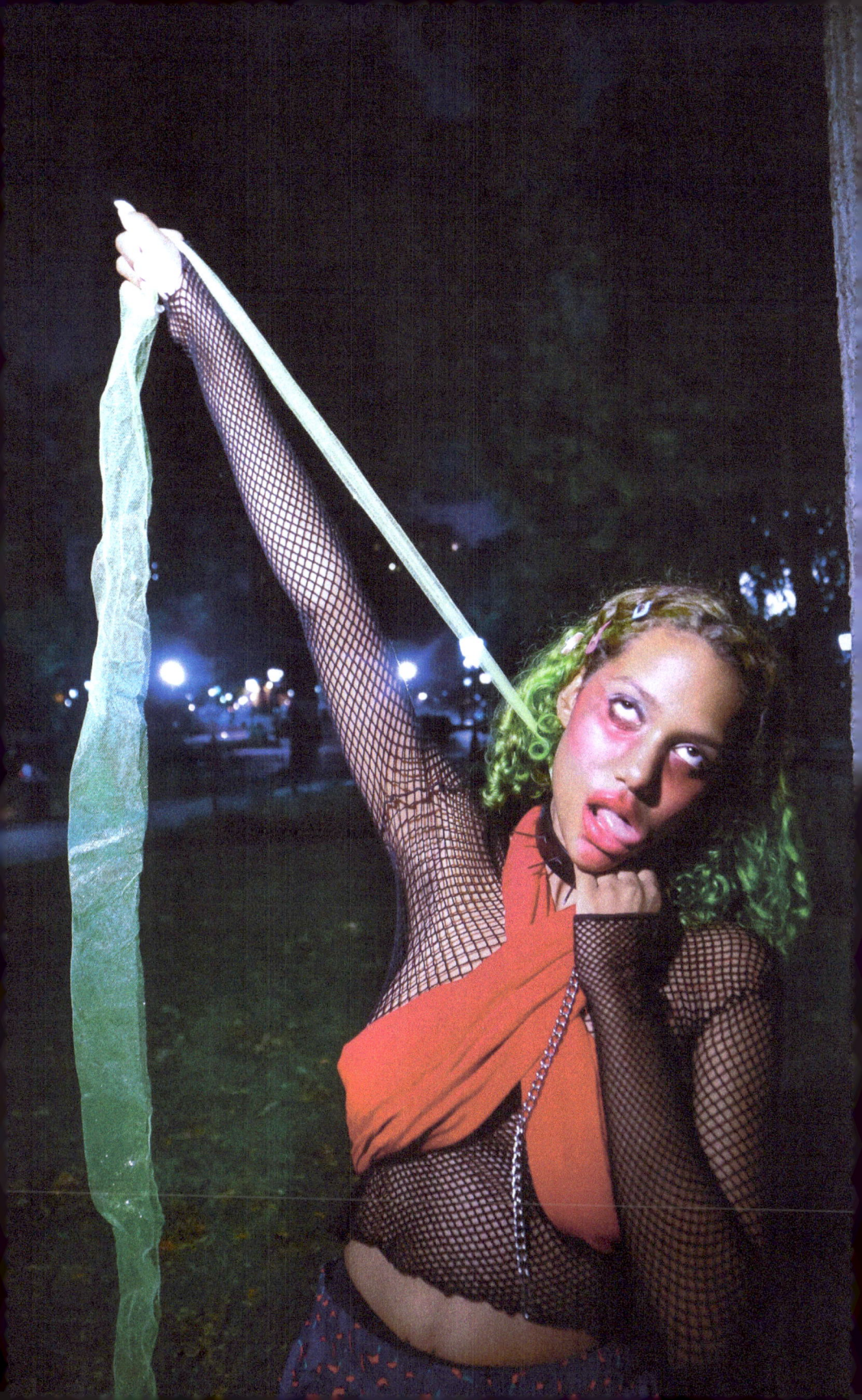

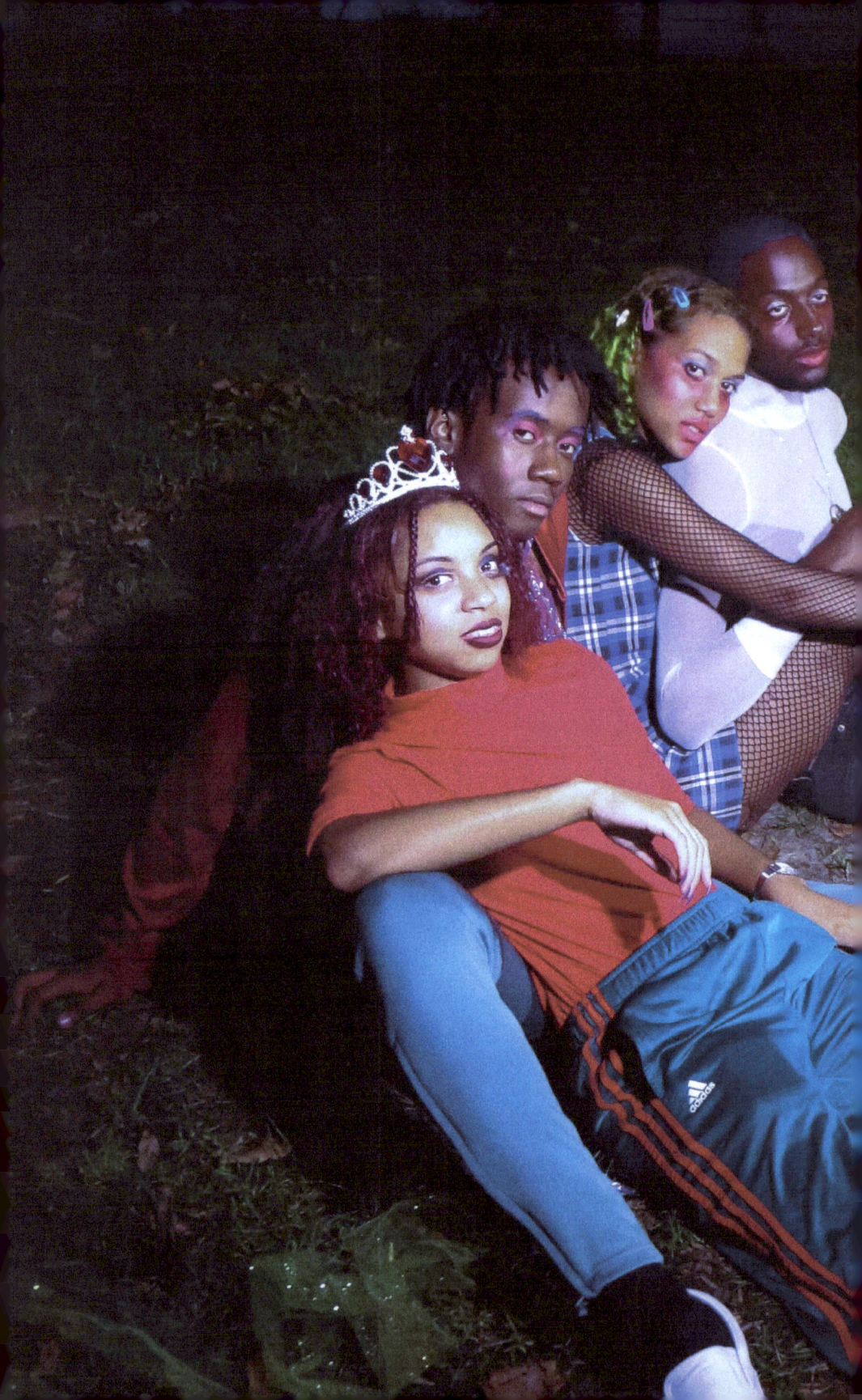

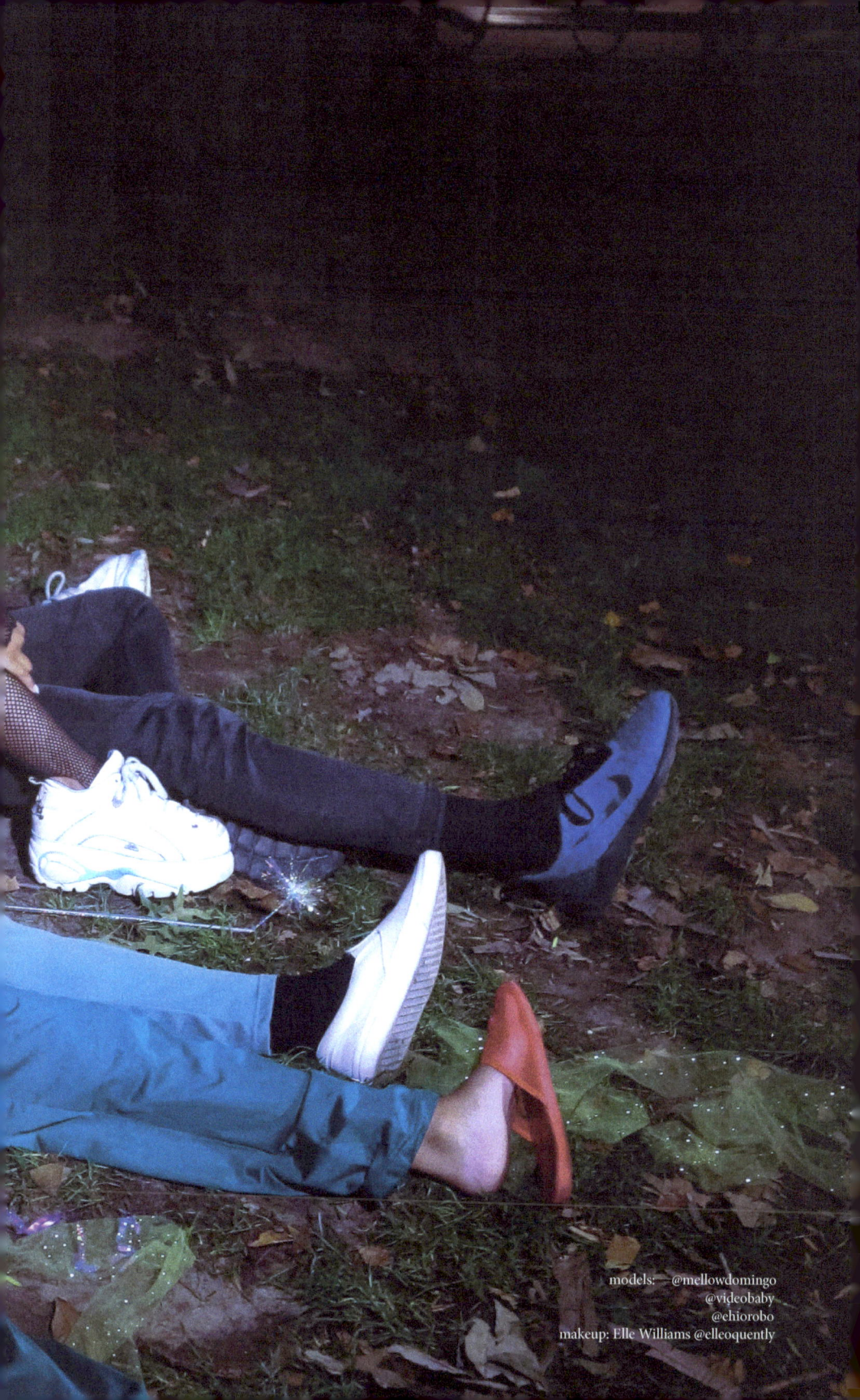

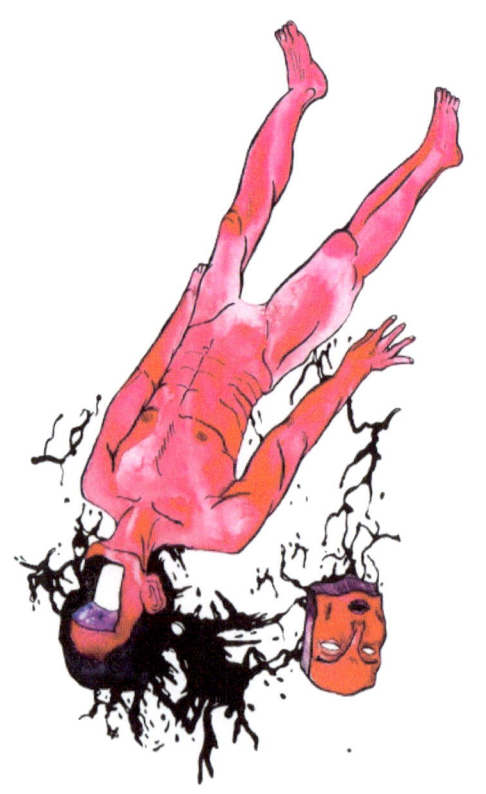

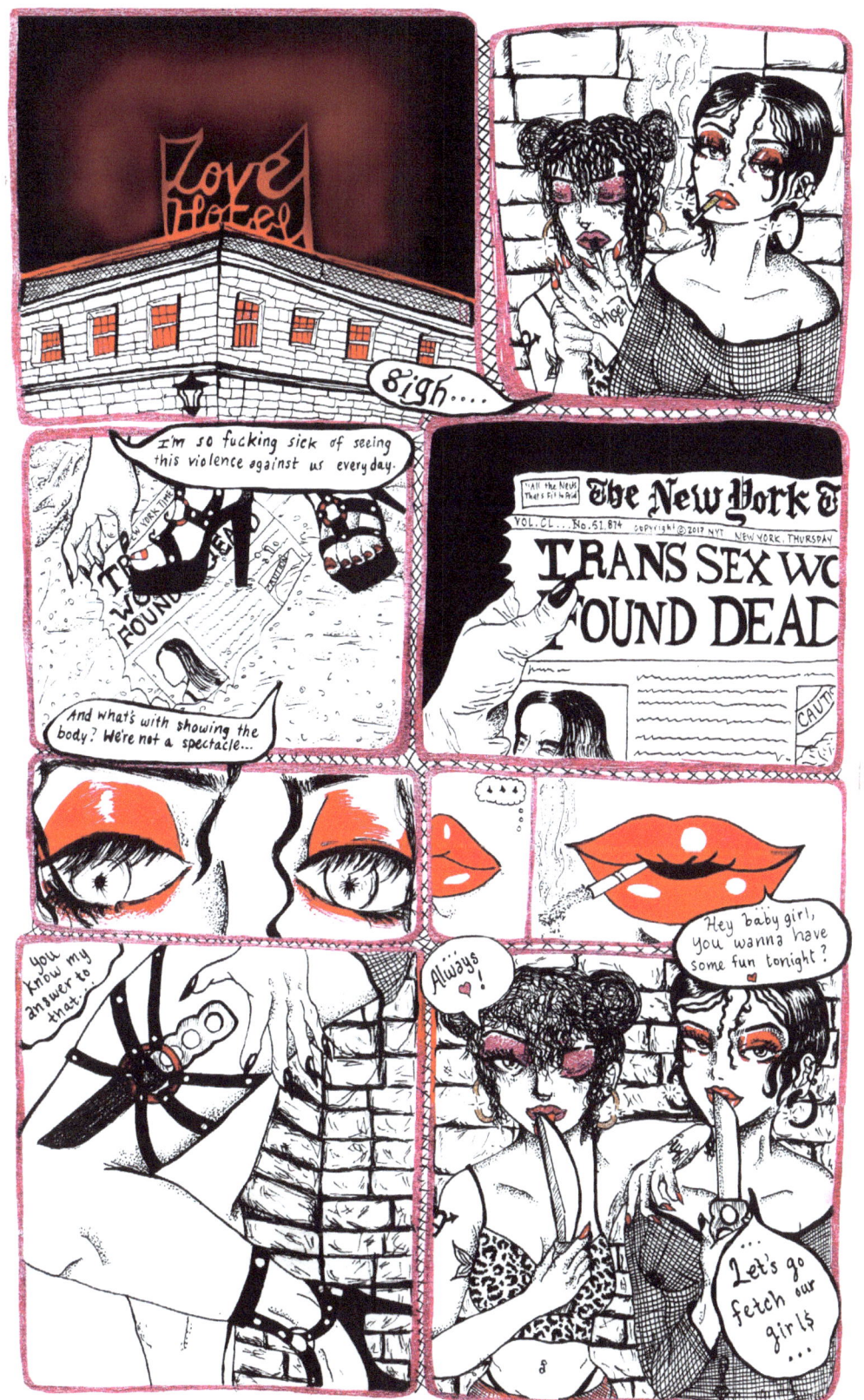

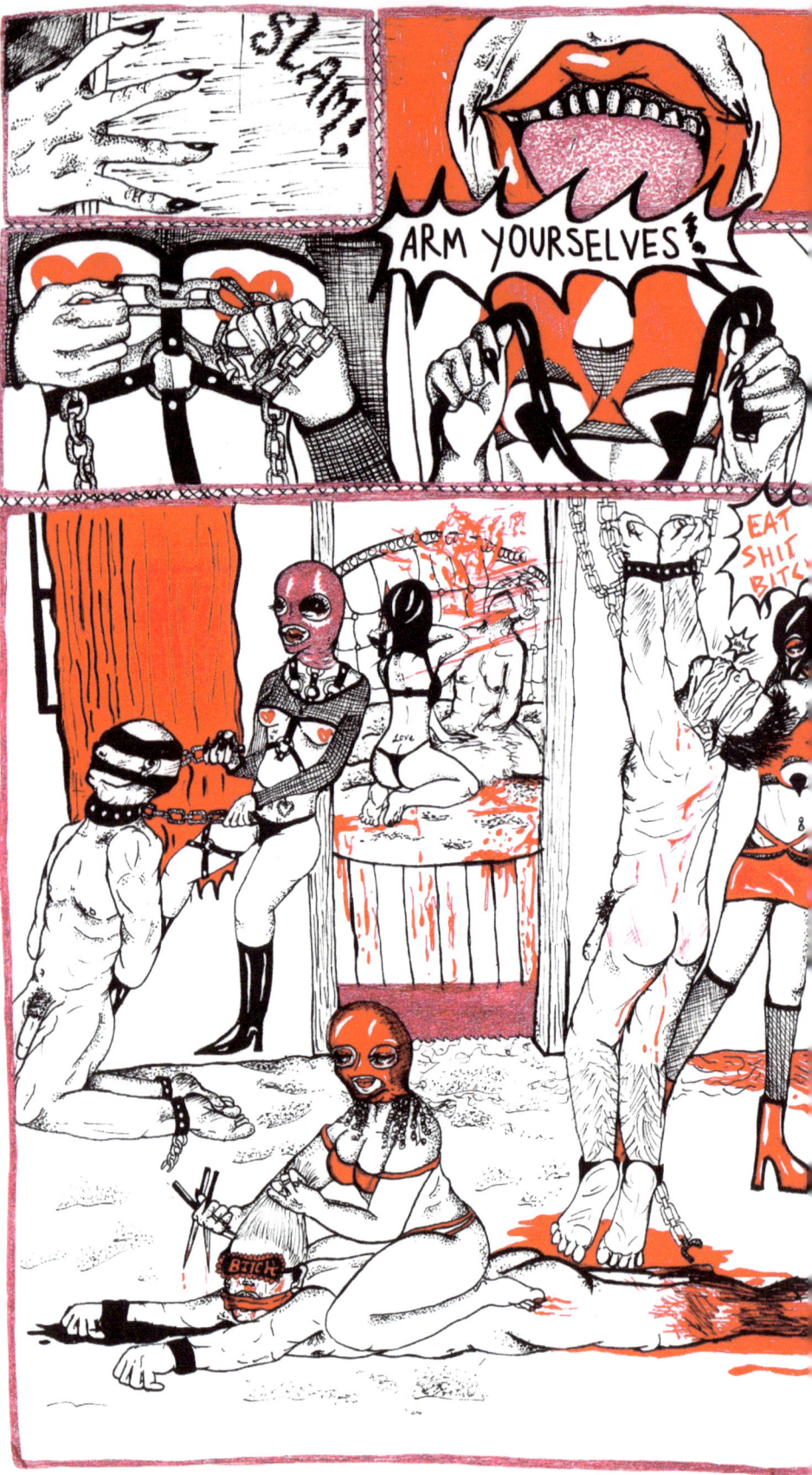

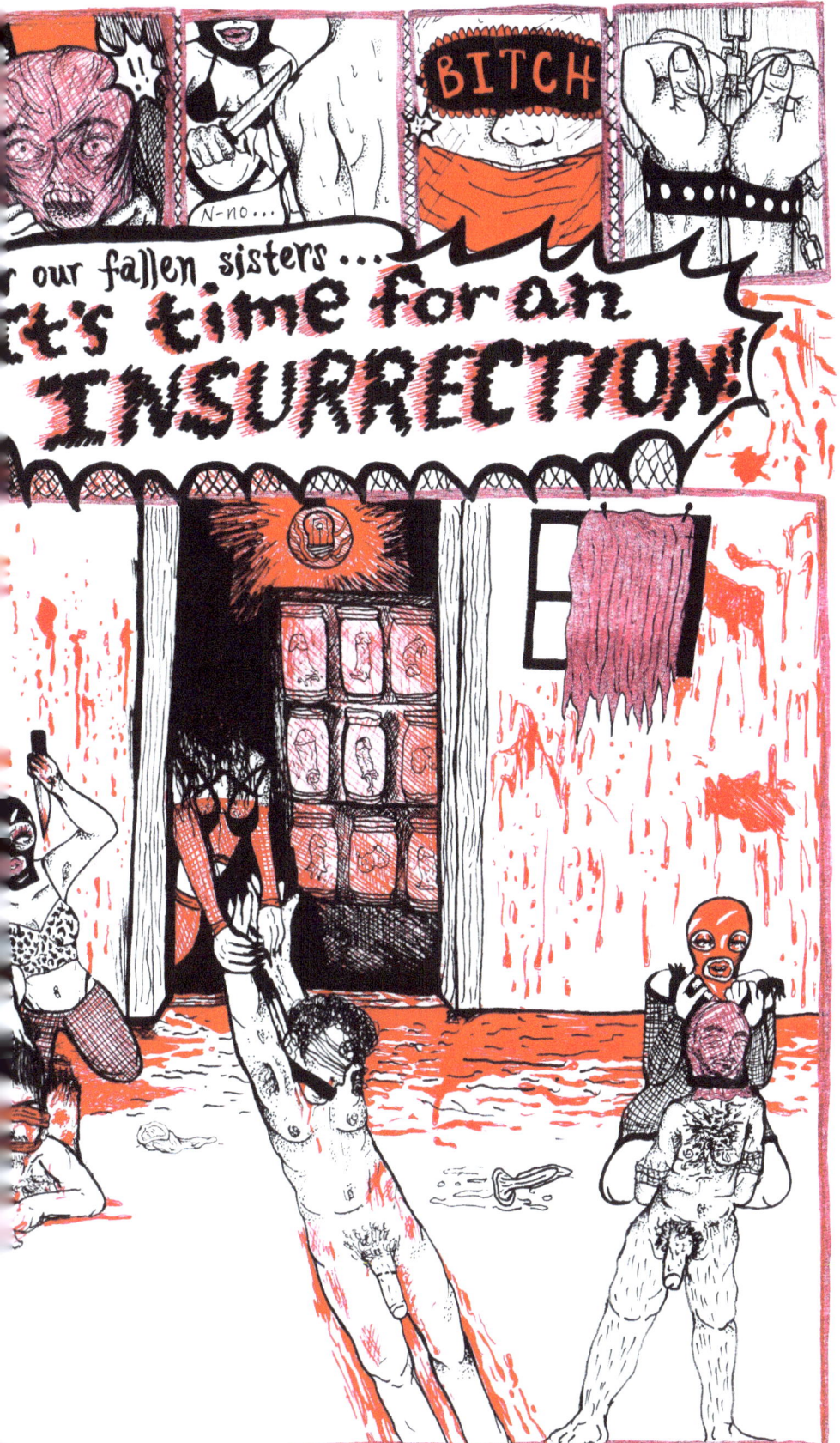

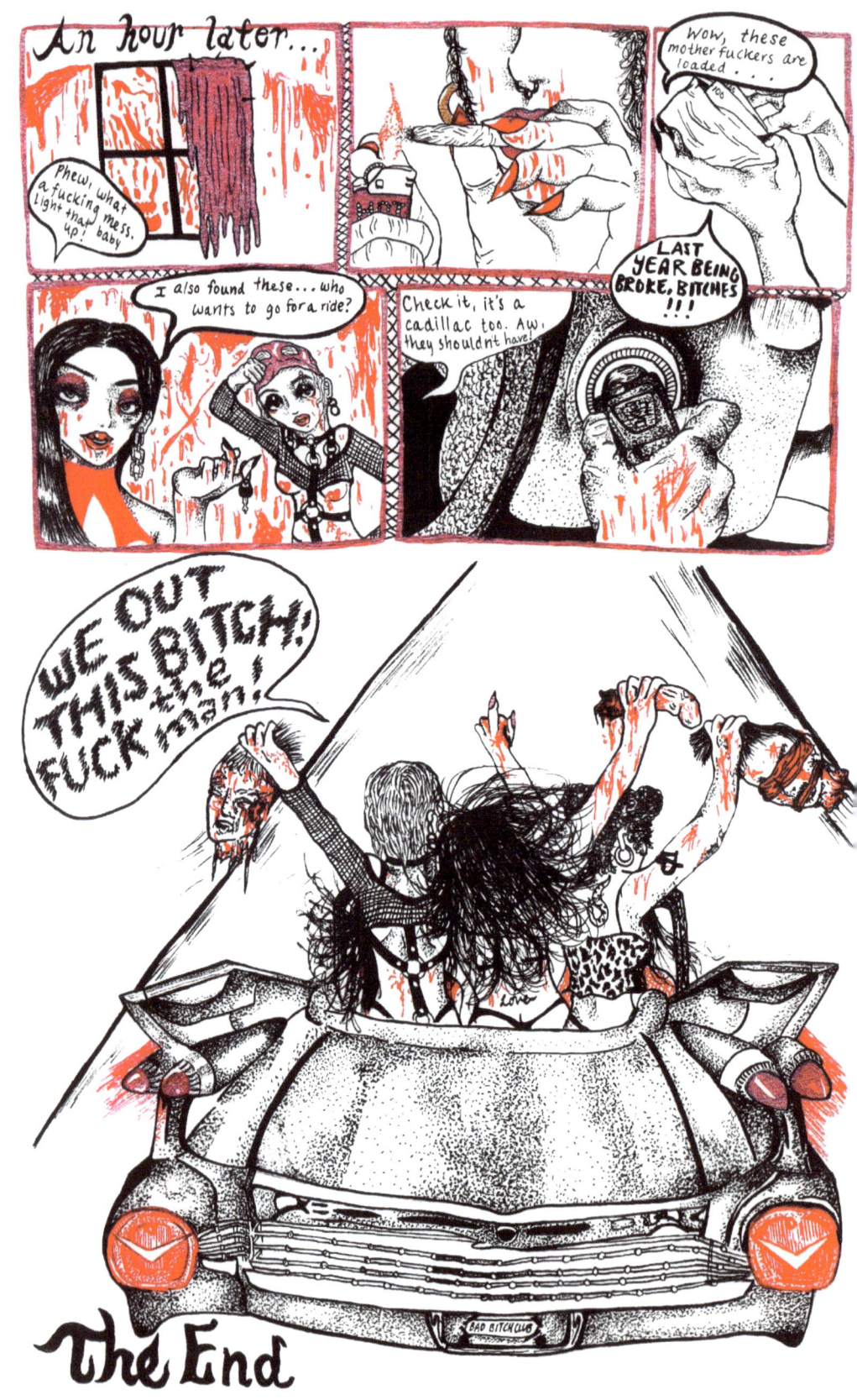

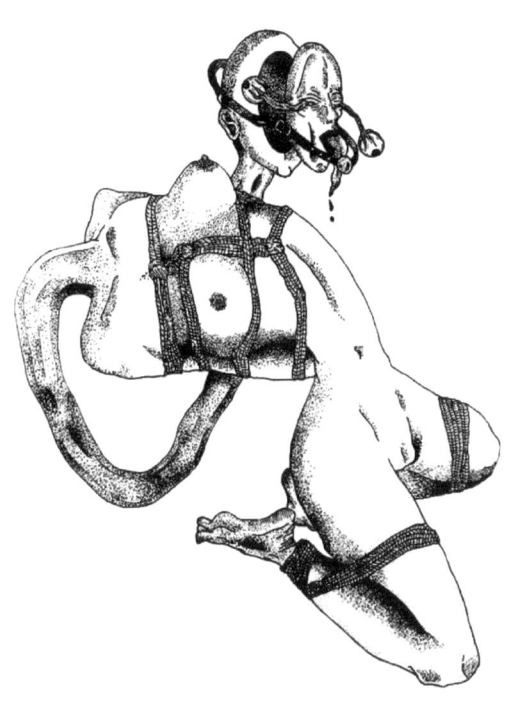

illustrated by: Annie Jin @deadgrips

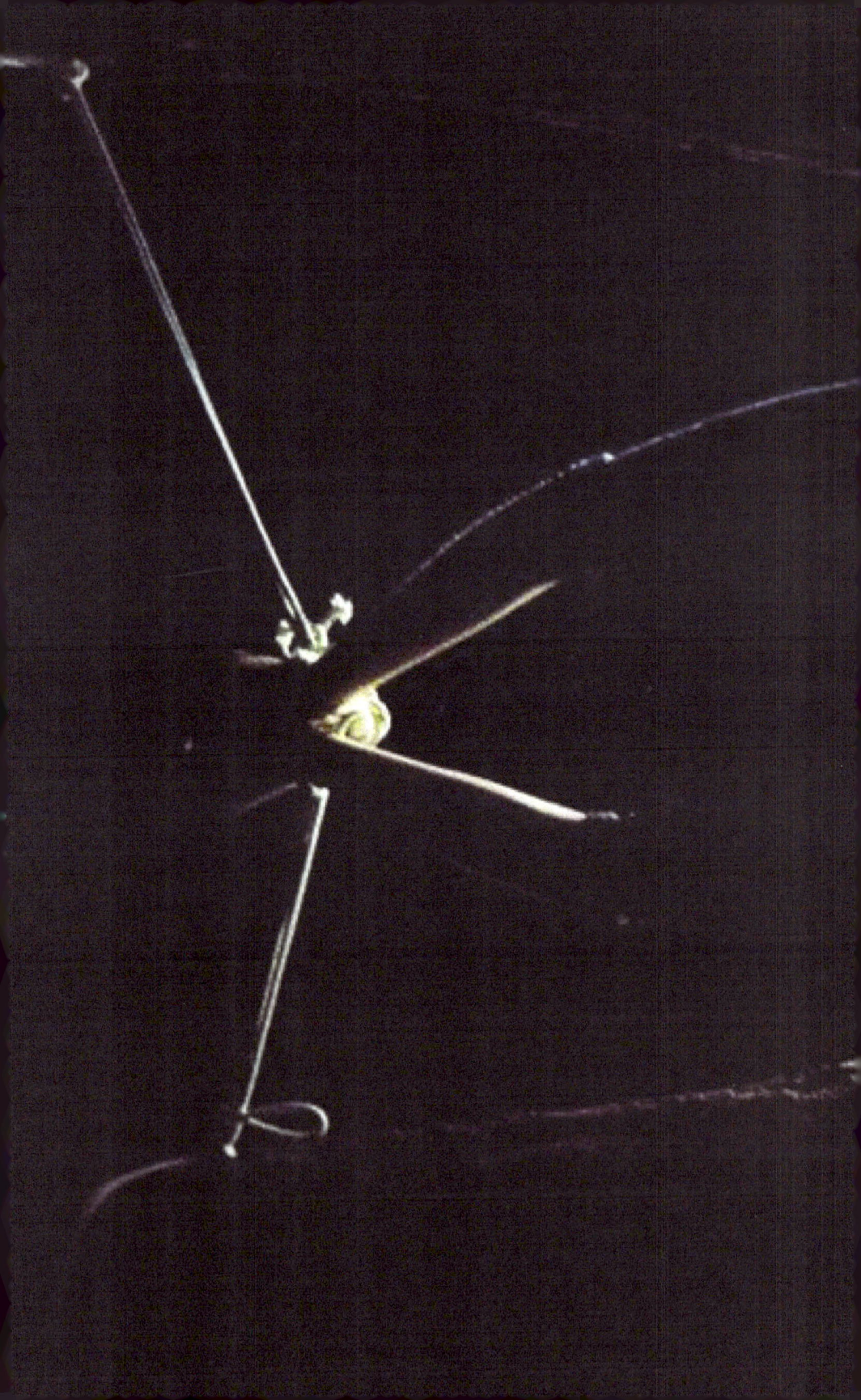

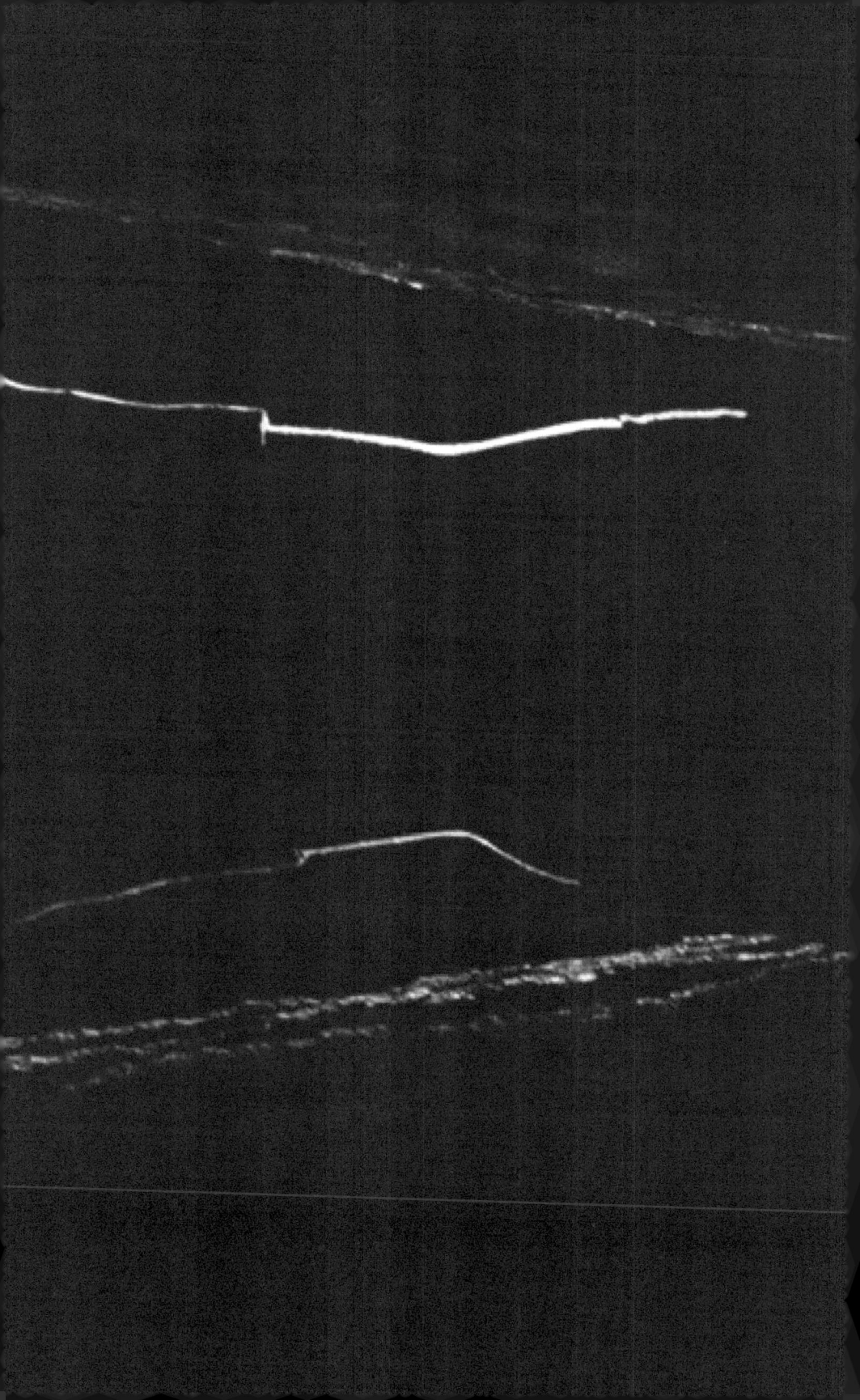

photographer: Isa Anais @videobaby
model: Adriana Artola @adriana_artola

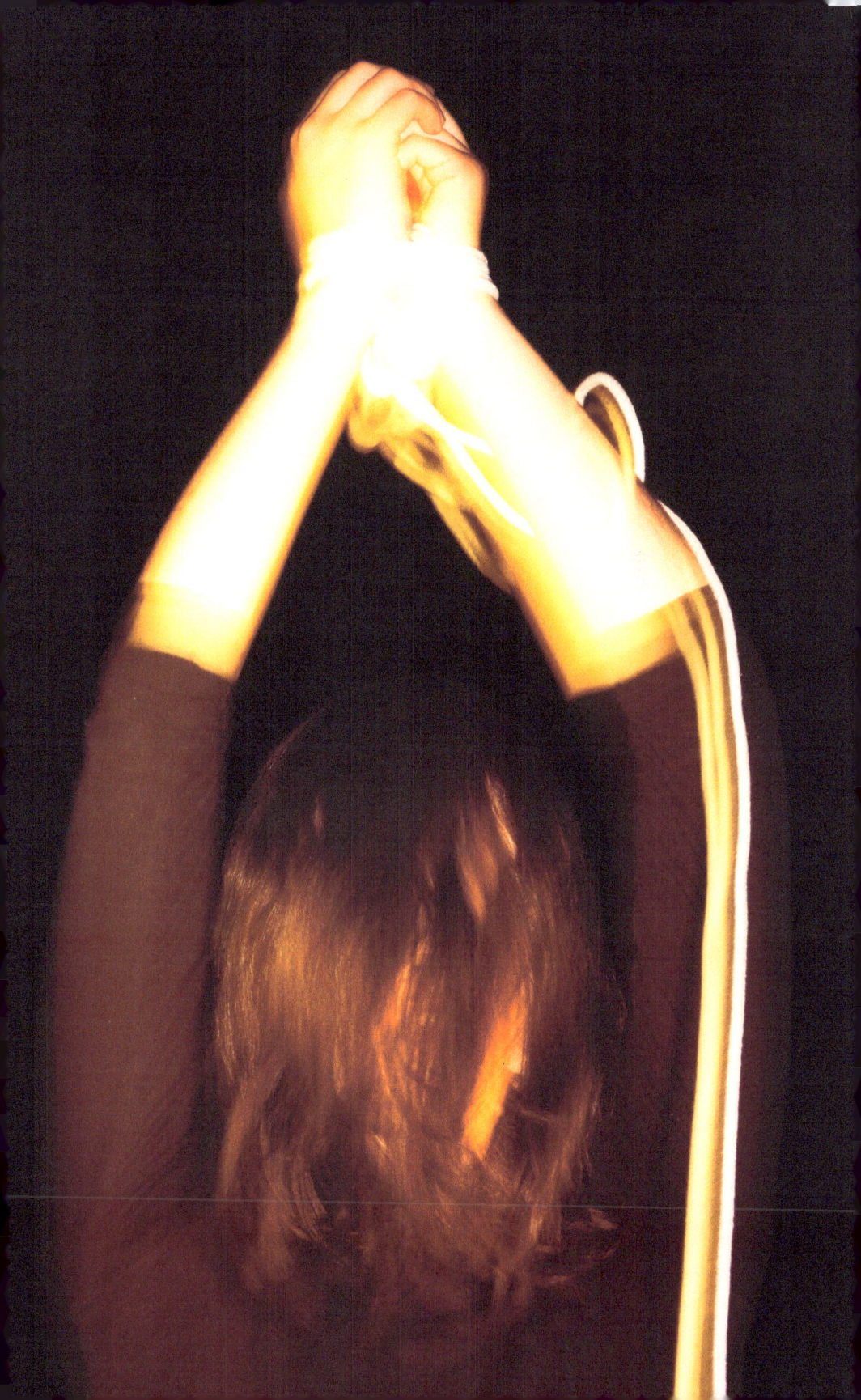

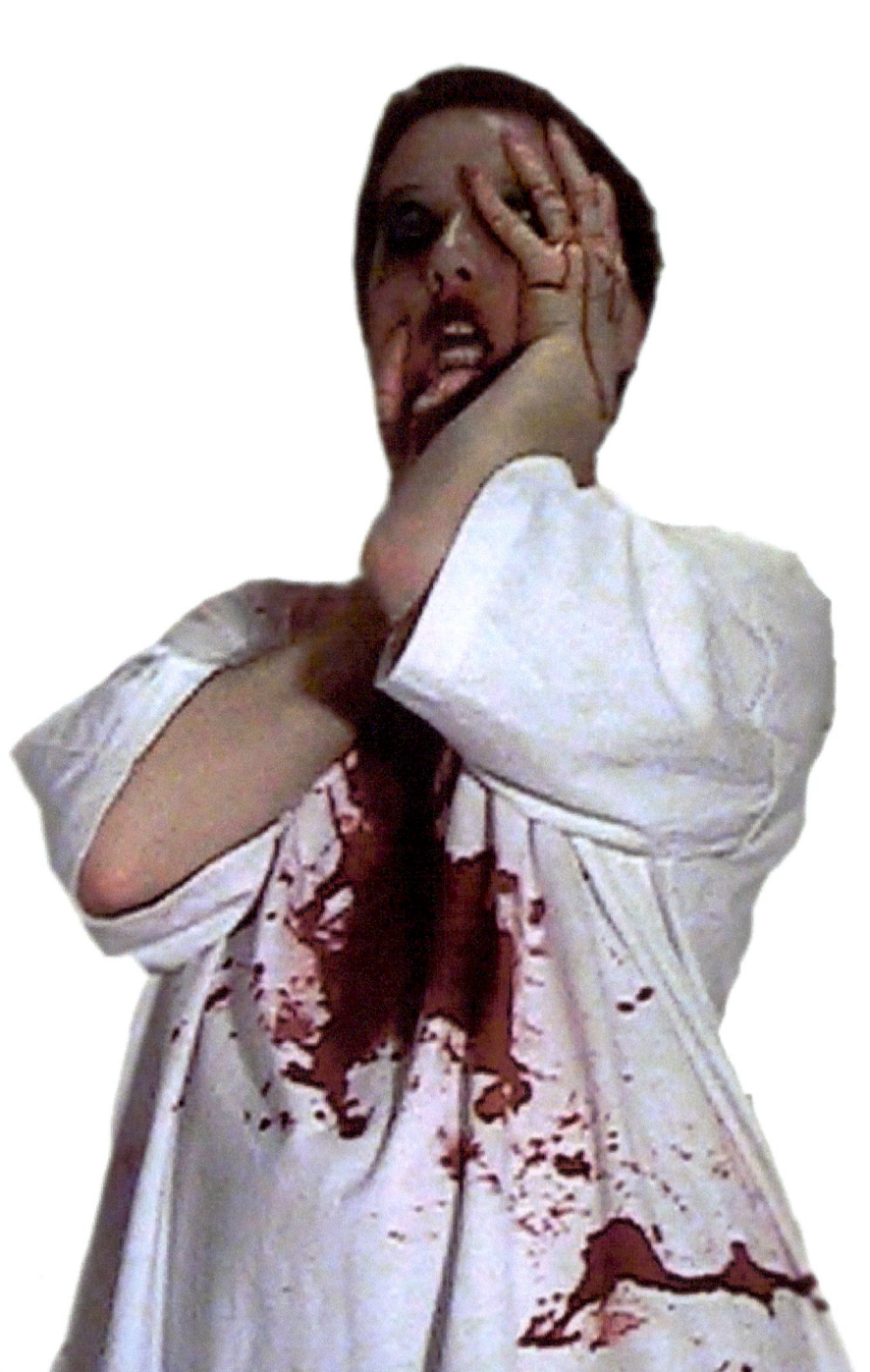

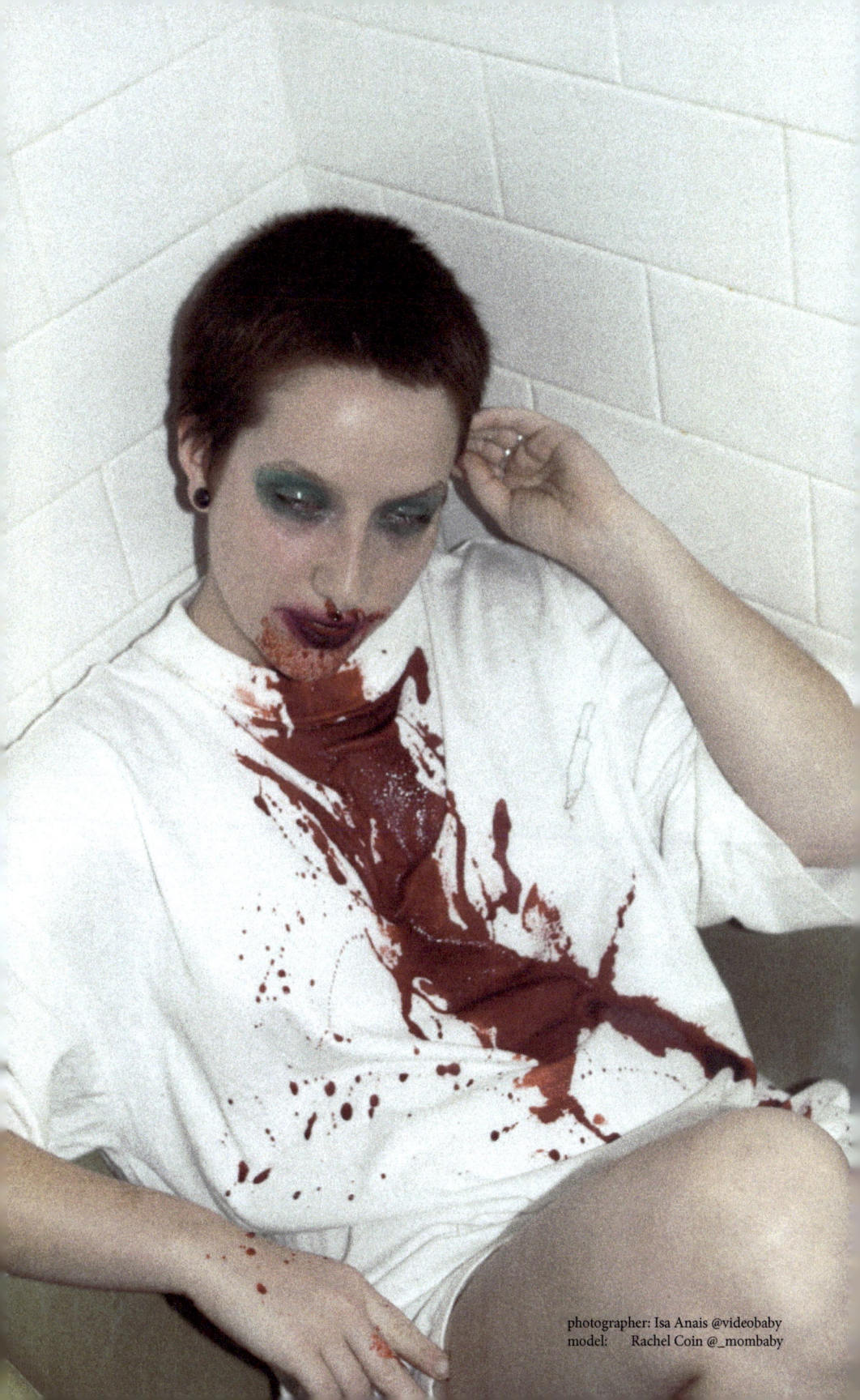

photographer: Isa Anais @videobaby
model: Rachel Coin @_mombaby

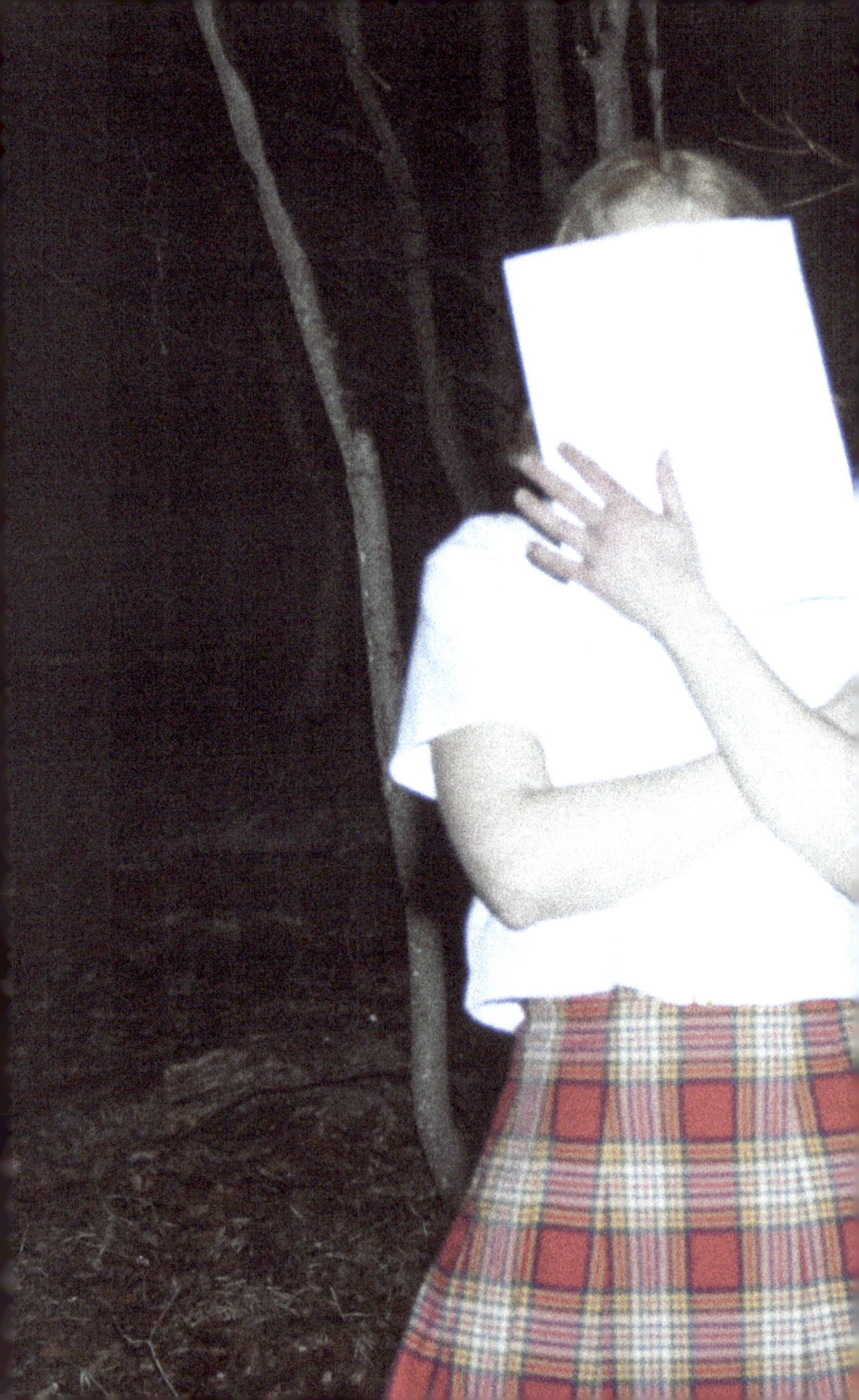

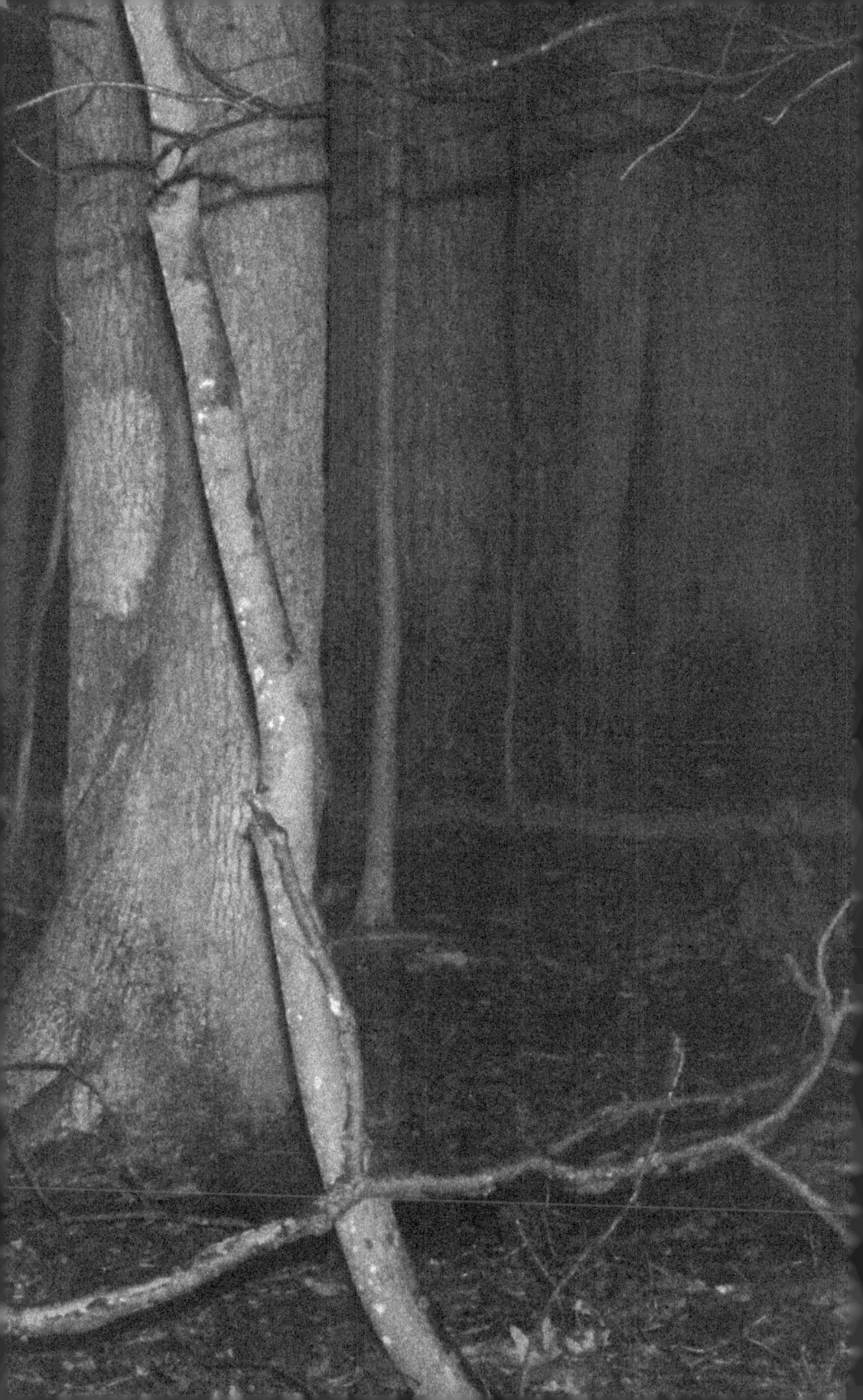

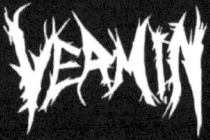

verminzine.com
@vermin.mag

www.ingramcontent.com/pod-product-compliance
Lightning Source LLC
Chambersburg PA
CBHW040227220526
45473CB00001B/149